# I *used* to *think* PEOPLE my *age* were OLD

# I *used* to *think* PEOPLE my *age were* OLD

Kathleen "Casey" Null

Bookcraft
Salt Lake City, Utah

*For my father, William Robert Hardy (1919–1993), who gave me the gift of a love for reading, writing, drawing, and imagining.*

Library of Congress Catalog Card Number: 95-76156
ISBN 0-88494-984-2

First Printing, 1995

Printed in the United States of America

# CONTENTS

# INTRODUCTION

In writers' classes they like to simplify the subject of novel writing by stating that there are only so many plots. It seems that novel writing is a complicated endeavor, and so perhaps students will feel a bit less overwhelmed if they can count the plots on the fingers of one hand. A typical list of plot types reads like this:

> The self versus the self
> The self versus another
> The self versus the state
> The self versus time/nature

The stages of our lives are also terribly complicated and can seem overwhelming (and sometimes they just *are* overwhelming). The stage that is the most complicated is always the one we happen to be in at the time.

Being in the "wasn't-life-supposed-to-have-begun-at-forty?" stage, I look back to my young adulthood and young motherhood and, in comparison, those stages seem like periods of relative leisure. Sure there were adjustments, hardships, and 3:00 A.M. diaper-and-bedding changes. But all the children could be tucked into their beds each night with a kiss and "one more" sip of water. I knew where they were and what they were doing. Most of the time I even knew what they were thinking or about to do.

The tuck-them-all-in stage is but a whisper of fond memory. I can't be totally certain about what teenagers are up to. Trust is a much more complicated concept than sure knowledge.

If the uncertainty involved with having teens was the only complication of the middle years, that would be enough stress. But the heat of the refiner's fire is turned up. There are financial fears, like, "Braces? You're saying that every one of them needs braces? And they cost *how* much? They can chew food, can't they? They won't starve, will they? If we get them braces they might, however." And there are employees being laid off by the thousands at the company where your husband is employed. The car radio keeps you informed about it on your way to the supermarket, where you'll discover that the per pound cost of apples has just gone up by another fifty cents—again.

And then there's gravity. The cost of living goes up, and our bodies go down. Well, let's not get into a depressing subject like bodies in the middle years; it can all be summarized thusly: However much exercise you needed to stay fit at thirty, multiply by 123,852 and that's how many hours of exercise are needed to achieve 40 percent of former fitness levels. However many calories and fat grams you consumed at thirty must now be cut to one-eighth. Simple enough?

In order to simplify a complicated life passage called "middle age" (can't someone find a better term?), I have decided to divide it into four sections that I have borrowed from novel writing classes (I knew I'd get *something* useful from those classes):

1. *The self versus the self.* We battle with ourselves as much as we battle with our teens, do we not? If not even more . . . as difficult as it may be to imagine.
2. *The self versus another.* There are plenty of "anothers" to complicate our lives by the time we get to this stage.
3. *The self versus the state.* The schools, HMOs, used car salesmen, and the IRS, right?
4. *The self versus nature.* Self-explanatory!

The middle years are not easy. It seems that just as we're becoming sure about what we value, we've got children who seem to have been put on earth for the sole purpose of questioning all values.

We watch what we eat with diligence and dutifully take our regular aerobics sessions, but we never look as slim and supple as our kids who sit around in front of the TV eating cheese puffs and Ding-a-Lings.

We are on the cutting edge: should we trust that we will gray gracefully and flatteringly, or should we color now, before it's too late?

We realize that it's definitely too late to do any more programming on most of our children, if not all of them; and we hope that we've taught them correct principles, and that they will soon govern themselves, say, by the time they're thirty.

Our kids ask us questions like, "Did they have paper plates when you were a kid?" Or if we should happen to sing along to a sixties rock song that has been made into a laundry detergent jingle, they will ask, "Oh, is that an old-fashioned song from long ago?"

So, the middle years have their challenges. There hasn't been a time when we are more in need of some solitude to sort things out. (I sincerely hope that I will *not* look back on this time as a period of relative leisure.) And there is never a time when we have less solitude.

Aging is an inevitability from which we cannot escape. But that doesn't mean we have to focus entirely on our increasing girth. And it also doesn't mean that we should give in to the dreaded disease of hurry-itis, which is so common in the middle years. At every stage, our lives are worth examining. Even these in-between years. I have found that these days my life slips through my fingers, weeks seeming like moments, years seeming like weeks. Someone once revealed to me that the secret to keeping life from being some kind of runaway train is in deliberately slowing it down, even stopping it from time to time. I have tended to attempt to save time by doing eight things at once, and by never, *never* doing nothing. But it's trying to do too much that causes life to slip out of our grasp. I once described it like this:

### Tack It Down

Life is like a satin ribbon
rushing.
It slips through
my fingers
cool and silky,
a blur of narrow fabric.
I can only see it clearly
When I stop
and tack it down
to hold it still
momentarily.

Then I see
the tiny stitches
along its careworn edge
and the sheen of the weave.
But I can't hold it
still.
I let go
and it becomes again
a rushing blur of satin.

# PART ONE

———— ❖ ————

# Whose Side Are You On Anyway?

*(The Self Versus the Self)*

Around middle age many of us notice that if we were to kick the person who has caused us the most trouble, we wouldn't be able to sit comfortably for several days. Why do we get in our own way so many times? Why is it that the deepest, most intense struggles seem to be the ones that take place within our own souls?

The struggle of the self versus the self is so universal that novelists write countless tomes on the subject. Perhaps they do so to avoid facing their own inner struggles. Admittedly, it is easy to lecture a teenager on why it is better to hang clothes in the closet after they are washed rather than to store them on the floor until they are needed and then to wash them. It is easy to talk about the weaknesses of another with great insight.

We might think that we can simply avoid all inner struggles while dealing with more compelling issues, like what to scrape together for dinner or how long to ground a son (the rest of his life? or just for the weekend?).

But when we avoid inner struggles, as we all do, they come up when least expected and bite us.

Or, we could go on and on thinking a certain way or doing things a certain way—cumbersome ways, no doubt—without realizing that not only is it unnecessary for us to be that way, it is slowing us down, limiting us, or even burdening us. If only we could see clearly enough, we'd be set free.

For instance, consider the tendency to adapt. It can be a good thing or it can be a cumbersome thing . . .

## *Fences*

I don't recall where I first heard this story or who first told it, but this is how it goes: A man, observing that his wife always cut off the end of a roast before putting it in the pan and then into the oven, became curious. For years he'd seen her doing this, but in the past he had always filed it away as one of those mysterious things that only women knew about. Now he became curious, and he couldn't see any logical explanation.

When he asked her why she cut the end off the roast she, too, had no logical explanation. The only answer she could come up with was that that was how her mother had always done it, so surely there must be a reason, but she'd simply forgotten it.

Later, when the opportunity presented itself, the couple asked the wife's mother about the practice of cutting the end off the roast. The mother looked blank for a moment or two, and then, as the light of understanding came to her, a smile also brightened her face. "Why, I *had* to cut off the end of the roast. I didn't have a pan big enough to hold it!"

So there was the explanation, as simple as that. She was adapting to the situation at hand. But adaptation continued even into the next generation, only it was adaptation for its own habitual sake. There was no reason for her daughter to continue to cut off the end of every roast.

I remembered that story because I'd met my brother and his family in Yellowstone one summer and he told me a similar story. He said that when Great Danes are puppies it is a common practice to enclose them in a fence that is just barely at a level they can't jump over. The puppies make many attempts to jump over the fence, but finding that they can't do it, they give up. As the puppies grow larger there is no need to replace the fence with a higher one, because even though the puppies could jump over it now if they tried, they don't try. They think they can't jump over the fence, so they don't.

These stories make me wonder how often we adults continue to limit ourselves because of past experiences or echoes of voices in our heads telling us that we can't do something.

We seem to be very skilled at adaptation, which is good.

But are we not sometimes too adaptive? And do we sometimes adapt mindlessly, needlessly, and often without awareness?

Adapting can also alter our perception. I discovered that while driving, as this experience illustrates:

". . . The car's been pulling to the right," my husband had been saying. "Have you noticed?"

"Huh? Oh . . . no, I haven't noticed." I even tried to notice the next time I was driving. Even with conscious effort I didn't notice. *It must be one of those male hormone things,* I thought. *Either men are sensitive to these little quirks that are related to wheeled and motored things, or they are quirky themselves and just think that the car is pulling to the right.*

I thought nothing more about it until later, when my husband began to say, "I need to take the car in for an alignment."

This I heard. But I barely understood it and I didn't have an overwhelming need to, so I forgot about it again.

I forgot until he began to ask, "What would be a good day this week to take the car in for an alignment?"

Then I had to pay some attention. I had to pick a day when I wouldn't need the car and could stay home, which had a certain appeal. The hard part was negotiating around dental appointments and expeditions to the supermarket.

When the day came I barely missed the car, as busy as I was. And so, when my husband brought it home at the end of the day, I was involved in making chili and never got around to asking him about the car.

The next morning, as I pulled into the 8:00 A.M. rush hour traffic by making a left turn onto a busy street, I noticed that the car definitely seemed to be pulling to the left. All the way to my destination I felt I had to consciously compensate for the car's apparent unwavering desire to veer left.

Then I remembered all those things my husband had been saying about the car pulling to the right. I hadn't noticed that the car was pulling to the right. It had come out of alignment so gradually that I had simply adapted to it just as gradually. But now that it had been aligned, I felt as if it were making sharp lefts. Had I overadapted to such an extent that normalcy now seemed abnormal? Are there any fences around me that I view as being so high they confine me, when in reality I could jump over them if I tried?

Imagined fences and limitations are not the only things that keep us from soaring. Sometimes it's our daily "to-do" list.

There is a complaint I frequently hear, and that is that so much time is taken up with such things as earning a living, doing laundry, and hunting down dust bunnies (complete with ears) that there is little or no time left to learn to play the piano, paint, write the great American novel, write a personal history, or breathe. If that weren't stressful enough, there's always the parable of the talents to consider. And I've often had a nagging feeling that although life is meant to be a time for testing and trials, it wasn't intended that we spend every second in duty . . .

### WHAT ARE YOU WAITING FOR?

Here it is, it's all yours.
Well, what are you waiting for?

But there's nothing here!

There is, I gave you plenty.

But it's all gone.

Well, where did it go?

It was all taken up.
Every necessary thing took long hours.

Just to live?

Just to live.

Did you live?

No.

Some of us middle-agers might look back on our more reckless times and feel that that was a time when we really did live . . .

## *Coward*

My friend Dina and I were talking about what daredevils we were when we were younger. I told her that my siblings and I would go into the ocean every day, even when tropical storms amplified the waves in size and power, churning the ocean into a kelp-laced experience in survival. I told her how I nearly drowned one September when, as I was relaxing in deep water, a sudden storm sent waves eight feet and higher rushing into shore, which sent the sunbathers scrambling. I, meanwhile, had to stay alive for what seemed like hours as the giant waves broke over and on me and sent me into deeper and deeper entanglement in the kelp beds, also brought to shore by the storm.

Fortunately it was the end of a summer of ocean swimming, and I was young, so I managed to remain calm and hold my breath for long periods of time. I might not be able to endure such an experience now that I am not so young.

But, we decided, I wouldn't put myself in such a position now anyway. I would not even think to relax by floating in the ocean beyond the breaking waves, with hurricanes busy off the coast of Baja California.

Dina told me that she used to ski jump off the edges of things and not think a whole lot about where she would land until it was time to. Today that very thought is the antithesis of relaxation. "I would never do that now!" she shudders. "Why is that?"

Why indeed? As we explored the concepts of careless bravado and caution, we realized that there came a time in each of our lives when we changed quite suddenly. We pinned that time down to the appearance of our first child. At its first coo we turned into cowards.

Up until that time we were invincible children of the universe. We climbed the tallest trees, and fell from some of them, flew all over the world with all we needed in one backpack, skateboarded, parasailed, mountain climbed, and lived with roommates from totally foreign cultures.

That was B.C. (before children). A.D. (after delivery) something very strange happened. Suddenly we were changed. We couldn't go anywhere without bags and boxes and huge folding contraptions. We thought about germs. We saw sharp edges and falls everywhere we looked. Suddenly life became a fragile blessing that could be altered, hurt, or taken.

"Is it some kind of hormonal thing?" my friend asked. Maybe, to preserve the species. Or is it because while giving birth we have to go so close to the veil to bring that life into its mortal existence? Or perhaps all those diaper bags and folding playpens make us realize that a helpless life is totally dependent on us. We, who once took flight so readily, become nest-bound.

"Mom!" my son says. "Come try my new skateboard!"

I think about it. I used to skateboard back in the days when a skateboard was a slab of wood upon which we would attach roller skate wheels. I used to skateboard on the BYU campus, in fact. I remember skateboarding from the top of Helaman Halls to the bottom, going around all the dorms and then, by the time I got to John Hall, zooming at such speed that I had to crouch. That was great. I respond, "Are you kidding? I'd hurt myself!"

"Aw, Mom, it's okay. Just go a little ways right here where it's nice and smooth. I'll hold your hand the whole time."

"No, I'm serious. It's too dangerous!"

He gives up and goes outside to tell his brothers that I'm too chicken. I begin to recall the time we went tubing in Provo Canyon my senior year. About fifteen of us climbed onto five inner tubes, connecting them with our legs. We took off down the icy slope at a ridiculous pace, hit a bump, and separately became airborne.

I smile as I remember. It was really fun. I guess we were just blissfully ignorant to the dangers.

I stop smiling and rush outside. I go to arrest the reckless behavior of my children, but something stops me. They are smiling. They are collecting memories of reckless abandon to savor in their middle age.

I decide I won't stop them, but I *will* stand nearby so I can throw myself to the ground as a barrier between their bones and the concrete if they need me.

Actually, there's probably very little I could do to protect them, other than to worry. And worrying is a pretty useless activity: a self-induced state of inertia. To a large extent, most of the angst I experience is self-induced. Well, quite a bit of it anyway. Sometimes it seems like my head is full of noise . . .

HEAD NOISE

Head noise,
Like a net full of
Squirming, lurching,
Frantic fish
In the middle of

A calm, turquoise
Sea.

There is a kind of calm that is available no matter what happens to us. It is like a calm turquoise sea. The first step may be in accepting the inevitability of pain. After that, a sense of humor ought to be helpful . . .

## Misery Is Optional

Life has always been full of disappointments, and it always will be. People we love will betray us, flake out, disappoint us, fail, and generally mess up. Minor things will go wrong consistently. Major things will go wrong inevitably. So, if it's just going to be one thing after another, why not lighten up and see the humor in things that exasperate, frustrate, and try us? Why not enjoy life and see it as an adventure? We may have good reason to be miserable, but is that enough reason to comply? Pain is inevitable . . . but misery is optional.

INNER GARDEN

The world is darkening,
There is a hard-edged ugliness
Seeping into each day.
There is contention, war,

immorality, hate,
greed, deception in an
ever-increasing supply.

There is loss, pain, suffering,
sorrow, hardship, hard work,
anguish, anger, setbacks, collapses.

There is no magic wand
to make it all go away,

But there is the heart and soul,
the inner boundaries
of the private self
which can be protected,
where a garden can grow
and thrive,
where sun can shine,
colors can delight,
giggles can resound,
serene breezes can blow.

It is the garden of
free will,
where one can choose
what seeds to sow.


In middle age we are left on our own to determine what seeds to sow. There is no film and no manual. I have yet to see a class titled "Getting the Most out of Middle Age, Once You Admit You Are There." But a manual would be so helpful . . .

## The Middle-Age Manual

If there were a manual, these might be just a few excerpts:
*Gray hair:* "Perhaps you've been searching, from time to time, for that first gray hair. Won't you be surprised when you discover a whole colony of them growing unnoticed in a spot you hadn't thought to look?"

*Abominal abdominals:* "After doing two hundred sit-ups a day for 365 days, you may be disappointed to notice that there is good news and there is bad news. The good news is that your abdomen will be rock solid. The bad news is that it will remain buried under a layer of jelly of some degree of thickness (depending upon how many pregnancies you had, or how much weight you gained during your wife's pregnancies). Do not be alarmed; this is perfectly normal for your age."

*Fatigue-induced compromises:* "There will be days when you will be so tired that you won't care what your family has for dinner that night. Don't be surprised if you find yourself serving Beanee Weenees or Pop-Tarts."

*Forgetfulness:* "There will also be times when you will be forgetful. Do not be alarmed. Forgetfulness in the middle years is not a symptom of early-onset senility. It is simply a symptom of circuit overload. Let's face it. If you're driving a kid to seminary at 5:30 A.M., after being awakened at 2:00 A.M. by his older sibling who forgot to take a key, and you're worried that another sibling may run off to get married instead of serving a mission, and your father is scheduled for a quadruple bypass but he's flown off to Tahiti to have some fun first, you're going to forget that you're driving to seminary, and drive to the grocery store instead."

So middle age brings with it many perplexing changes. At least, as we fall apart on the outside we can count on getting it together on the inside, where it really counts.

I once knew someone who was full of uncertainty concerning both her outer and her inner beauty. As a result, she became obsessed with perfecting her environment with the things she placed in it . . .

SAFETY IN ACCUMULATION

She arranges her accumulations
About her person,
Once she has them perfectly placed
She goes out in a flurry of chatter
to find some more

Dainty or whimsical objects
to admire, she knows
Exactly where they would look perfect
With flounces and flourishes
and the perfect touch of color.

Her person is also
Arranged with an eye for
Perfection in surface details.
All looks well,
Except that her body
is a bulging container full
of festering turmoil
Kept within the boundaries
Which she has set
of flourishes and
Dainty details
Accumulated and arranged
About her person.

### SAFETY PART II

Her eyes are constantly darting from one object
To the next.
She is her things, her things are perfect,
Therefore, so is she.
She keeps her energy outside of herself,
Relentless, ever vigilant.
A force field that surrounds and never rests.

She dares not stop long enough to meet herself,
The core of her being.


Some camouflage pain with the distraction of accumulating. Some just scream . . .


## *Pain*

It was an ordinary kind of day. There was the homework—the kids' and mine—the chauffeuring, the usual stuff.

Then my youngest two went into the backyard to play. They were leaping into the air, grasping the horizontal bar across the top of the swing set and swinging outward to land on their feet. They were being a cross between gymnasts and monkeys.

I could see them from the kitchen window where I began my nightly ordeal: deciding what to create for dinner that would be offensive to the least number of people. I didn't see the actual event, but I heard the cry that came from my daughter. It was one of those cries that instinctively alert the mom. This was not one of those typical boo-boos. This was serious. I rushed out the door to see my daughter attempting to get up from the dust, and helped her inside. When she sat down I saw that there was a peculiar bend to her forearm. Even with her three older brothers and my tomboyish tendencies, I had never experienced a broken limb before. But I was fairly certain that my time had come. My daughter wailed like an otherworldly banshee while I rushed for the ice and a pillow to support her arm.

When my husband walked in the door a few moments later he could see by the look on my face that this was not a bruise I was taking care of. And if that weren't enough, there's the fact that I said, "We need to take her in to urgent care."

The X rays confirmed that she had broken her wrist. And then we discovered that her pain would be prolonged. Our HMO had to send her to another location, the next day, for a cast. So she went home splinted, wrapped in an Ace bandage, and whimpering.

After a restless, painful sleep she endured yet more X rays, which caused her to break out in a cold sweat. Finally, with a pink and white cast and a Snoopy sling, I brought her home. In the quiet she solemnly shared with me the extent of the pain she had experienced.

I understood because I had watched it all and had wished that I could have traded places with her.

A few nights after that my daughter was poking pipe cleaners and chopsticks down her cast to get the "itchies," and my youngest son was experiencing another kind of pain.

He had made plans to have a friend come and stay

overnight. This son is a highly sociable being, a fact which causes his more introverted parents to scratch their heads in wonder. For him, a friend coming to spend the night is right up there with a trip to Disneyland. He was so excited that he seemed to be running from floor to wall to ceiling to other dimensions and back again to tell us how excited he was.

But things don't always turn out like we want them to, and we tried to tell him that, but he was too distraught to hear it when his friend couldn't make it after all. He suffered an anguish similar to his sister's, only his was emotional. I wished I could create some kind of friend out of unorganized matter for him. It would be a friend who was as enthusiastic about life and sleep-overs as my youngest son. And this creation would come immediately to the door to ease this son's suffering.

As I comforted these two with their pains I realized that all the words I had to offer could only soothe through vibrating tones. They were too young to understand that these pains were fleeting, though painful. Some words I said only to myself: *If only these things could be the most painful things you ever experience in your lives.*

And then I thought of how much pain I had suffered to that point. As large and engulfing as those experiences were, they were still such a small fraction of what He suffered for me. I wished to trade places with my daughter when she broke her wrist, knowing it would be painful. But that's not such a sacrifice when compared with the suffering He undertook for all of us. Our painful experiences teach us, strengthen us, and give us compassion for the pain of others, but they only give us a tiny glimpse of what was suffered for our sakes.

We are like children, whimpering and wounded and only partially seeing the big picture. But perhaps the time will come when we will understand, and gratitude will replace the pain.

And in the end, things always seem to work out for the best. I didn't have to cook dinner that night, after all.

It's not easy to go around with an attitude of gratitude when adversity strikes, because we are mere humans, tiny children in the eternity of things. So it might be asking too much for us to immediately feel gratitude. Imagine hearing, "So, my son is flunking algebra; and I will need one of those medical tests, you know, the ones that are really painful; and our house is so badly cracked from the earthquake that we'll have to move out. I was already feeling really grateful that the refrigerator quit and my car was rear-ended and I got whiplash . . . but now my cup runneth over!" When was the last time you heard someone talk like that?

Oh well, if we must postpone our gratitude during hard times, at least we can find lots of other things to appreciate even while we are being abundantly blessed with challenges . . .

## *Thank You*

I was going through a truly rough time. I don't recall which one it was. I stepped outside feeling bent from the weight of my particular burden and was startled by the sudden colorful flurry of a butterfly that seemed to be trying to get my attention by flying directly in front of my face.

I couldn't help but stop to watch. The butterfly continued to flutter before me; then it soared into the sky. I looked up, watching the air show, noticing the blue sky. Then I thought it was over, but the butterfly floated back down and stopped on a leaf in front of me. It spread its wings in the sun. I continued to watch, forgetting my troubles for a moment, visually exploring the patterns on the wings. Then, after a good long look, the butterfly began its dance again. It nearly seemed to express happiness as it flitted from one point to another.

I stared at the three where I'd last seen the butterfly and said aloud, "Thank you!" Then I picked up my burdens (which seemed just a bit more manageable) and went on.

The feeling that I had been presented with a gift never left me. I've noticed since then that gifts often come at unexpected moments. Sometimes they come when I really need something. Sometimes they simply come, no strings attached.

One summer day when my two youngest children were about nine and six years old, they were playing in the front yard. The sun was getting close to the horizon, and I went to the window to call them inside for dinner. But when I got to the window I didn't call to them, because there was a gift for me. The sun had backlit the grass so it glowed. And there, on the glowing, bright green embers, pranced by barefooted children. Their hair seemed to be taking over for the setting sun. It, too, glowed, golden halos around their heads. And it streaked as they ran and somersaulted. I remained still, using my gift in the moment.

One busy morning I walked along the beach reciting my tight schedule for the day to make sure I didn't miss anything. I watched the surfers and thought I saw one who seemed to be in a good position to catch the wave, but then, instead of riding the face of the wave, he seemed to disappear into it. I saw this happen again and again and became curious. As I got closer I realized it wasn't a surfer at all. Well, it was, but not a human one. It was a dolphin. I was contented with this gift, but there was more. As I continued walking north along the shore I saw dozens of dolphins all lined up inside the waves.

It was a sight I can't forget. A wave would rise up, sleek and shining in the sun, an offshore wind blowing mist off the crest of the wave, and the wave would be full of bodysurfing dolphins, all lined up, striping the waves in formation. They'd all take the same angle as they rode the wave. Then they'd swim back for the next one.

I continued walking, but I was saying, "Thank you!" aloud. I looked toward the north and saw what appeared to be a rocky part of the beach. *That's so strange,* I said to myself (silently this time); *I don't remember there being rocks in this part of the water.* I had been in the water at that location hundreds of times and I knew there were no rocks there, but I was willing to accept any changes nature wished to thrust upon me. After all, this was earthquake territory.

Getting closer still, I saw one of the "rocks" spout. It was a whale! I walked much faster and soon realized it was a California gray and her calf. Then I got worried. It was May, and the gray whales were supposed to have migrated north by now. This whale and her calf might be in some kind of trouble.

I stopped near two fishermen who were watching peacefully. I asked them if anyone had called the American Cetacean Society. They didn't speak English. I went to a father and his little girl. He was watching with a smile on his face and his girl sat on his shoulders, her face full of wonder. I mentioned my concern to him. He said that it was because of El Niño, which changed the weather. The ocean was warmer. Whales were lingering and playing along the coast longer. He told me of seeing another whale and her calf playing just a couple of weeks earlier in the same place.

So, it was another gift. But I was too busy wondering if it had a warranty to enjoy it. Fortunately the whales lingered. They rolled in the surf. They batted each other with their fins. They slapped their flukes at surfers, showering them in salty waterfalls.

Soon the whales began to swim northwest in order to clear the Palos Verdes Peninsula before heading north again. I walked along the shore for as long as I could see them. When there was no more sign of them I stopped to look at the horizon and to say, "Thank you."

Daily gifts are not always that spectacular. They are often overlooked. For instance, when I have a morning when I just wake up gradually with the sunrise, instead of jarringly with an alarm, that's a gift. When one of my kids spontaneously gives me a hug and says, "I love you, Mommy," that's a gift.

Other gifts: A letter in the mail from a friend, seeing a car painted in a particularly interesting color, clean towels freshly folded, a bicycle ride, hearing a wind chime in passing, a baby's smile, seeing an eagle in flight, a giggle, a bird's nest, green lights all the way to church, the smell of fresh bread, getting a grass stain out of white jeans, seeing a single sailboat in the distance, a good book, a bird right by the window, freshly squeezed orange juice, seeing a fuzzy caterpillar (outside), a child's voice saying, "Wake up, it's morning!", an idea, a spontaneous pillow fight, rippled pink clouds, a shooting star, life.

One year I made some sacrifices and some others did the

same on my behalf so that I could attend the LDS writers conference on Oahu. Going to Hawaii was, of course, a gift, but that's obvious and also planned. There were many unexpected gifts waiting for me there, however. The one I recall the most was one night, feeling especially sleepy, still recovering from jet lag, relaxing in my room with the windows and doors all open, the lights all off. A cool breeze floated through the room; the curtains swayed gently. The breeze was scented with the tropical flowers that were everywhere. Some native Hawaiian men had gathered nearby and were talking. The sounds of the Hawaiian language continued for a while, and then the men began to sing old Hawaiian songs. They sang for hours, their voices forming a soothing harmony. The combination of the scented breeze and their voices was almost unbearably wonderful. "I must be in heaven," I said drowsily. And then, "Thank you."

I don't have to go to Hawaii to find my gifts (though that would be the preferred method). I don't have to go anywhere at all. No matter where I am, they find me. All I have to do is pay attention.

We also need to pay attention as we grow and gain more light . . .

### THE MAN-BOY

The Man-Boy,
Picking at the shell
That has contained him,
Safe and solitary—
He is almost free,
The opening widened
by his efforts.

But the shell contains
More than himself.
Pain was also kept
Within its walls,
A silent roommate.
It oozes over the edge,
Causing hesitation

and fear.
Will it drown him?
Will he slip on it?

He rests in the shell,
Looking one more time
At what has contained him,
Seeing it now
In the light
He has let in.


We need each other because we help each other grow. But there are times when we need to be alone for the kind of growth that can only occur in solitude . . .

## *Wilderness*

Our family held a reunion in a large cabin in the mountains overlooking the Utah Valley. We are Californians who truly enjoy spending time off in Utah, to get away from all the tourists who crowd into our state (some of whom are, I know, Utahns) each summer. And we like Utah. Especially the mountains.

My husband couldn't get time off from work this time, so while he was at home, working his way through the tourists each morning, the kids and I were experiencing another kind of crowding: cousins. They were everywhere.

It was sometimes difficult to arrange any kind of schedule with so many of us being hungry at the same time, or wanting to hike or swim at the same time (for some reason, this sameness was not in effect when it came to sleeping).

There was a nice swimming pool a few miles down a trail. One day all the cousins wanted to go immediately, including my own children. But I had just come back from someplace and wanted to eat lunch first, so they set off without me. I said I'd join them as soon as I ate.

When it was time to go I found that there were no other relatives willing to accompany me down the trail. It could be that there might've been at least one who had planned to go with me, but once the cousins had all left, they were enjoying the quiet so much that they felt they should cling to it. It might not come again for many days.

So I prepared my backpack and laced up my hiking boots and brushed aside the warnings that I shouldn't hike alone. It was only a few miles. It was a wide trail. And it was Utah, after all. Somehow I always seem to feel safer in Utah, as if there are even fewer rattlesnakes there.

I was confident that it would be just a short jaunt and that it was really no big deal. Besides, I'm an experienced hiker, as long as I can stay away from those goat trails that are three inches wide and cut into the side of a steeply sloping mountain with a four-hundred-foot drop on one side. I stepped outside and was met by the beauty of wildflowers and squirrels; everything would be fine.

Wouldn't it? Once I was a little further down the trail I wasn't so sure. For one thing, it was so quiet. I had never "heard" so much quiet before. I'm used to hiking with my family, who sometimes make a great deal of noise to keep bears off the trail. I knew a little noise would be a good idea. I began to make loud sounds with my hiking boots. But I felt like the woods on either side of the trail were full of wild animals and that they were all watching me. I didn't necessarily feel that they would attack me. Just the thought that they'd be watching me was a creepy feeling. The lone hiker being tracked by thousands of wild eyes.

I thought I ought to sing. I didn't know what to sing at first. I began to think of all the things that could happen and why a person should not hike alone. They could have an allergic reaction to an insect bite. They could disturb a rattlesnake with an attitude. They could slip and sprain an ankle. They could have a heart attack. They could have an anxiety attack. What if a rabid bobcat should be following them?

I was pretty far down the trail by now. Too far for anyone to hear me yell, I thought with some apprehension. Even though I grew up in an area that exposed me to plenty of wildlife (yes, Southern California was once that way), I began to think like a citified yuppie: *A bear will surely eat me. Maybe this hiking alone is not such a good idea.*

I was being too quiet. *Will the animals scamper away if I make noise, or will that simply alert them to my position?* I decided to cover all the bases. I began to sing hymns. So there I was, hiking away, my backpack thumping against my back, singing "I Am a Child of God" in a barely audible voice.

Just then there was a huge crack in the underbrush to my left, and onto the trail bounded a large stag. He stopped dead and we faced each other, inches away. I looked into his eyes and he into mine. I could see the fear in his eyes. I, on the other hand, felt no fear, though I thought I would. Instead, I felt amazement. I was enthralled. And I felt compassion that this creature had obviously not expected to confront a human being. I wanted the moment to last, but immediately he reared back and took off into the forest on my right.

I stood there for a moment, recovering from the suddenness of it all. Then I felt exhilarated. I continued down the trail with renewed vigor, singing "I Know That My Redeemer Lives" at the top of my lungs. The tension of fear of the unknown that had been building had been released by the known.

I have never forgotten my lone hike through the wilderness. It almost seems as if it was meant to be there, in my memory. I'm glad all those relatives wanted to stay in the quiet cabin. But would I do it again? Not a chance. What if that had been a grizzly sow instead of a stag? I'd still be at the top of the nearest tree.


One of the paradoxes of middle age is that while sometimes we can hike alone and feel good about it, we sometimes get conflicted over silly little things . . .

## *The Watch*

Life is full of paradoxes, and it seems that most of them concentrate around the middle (kind of like the extra pounds) of life. Middle age is a complex time. Our children ought to be more patient with us. It's a time complicated by paradox.

For instance. I had always wanted a *good* watch, as opposed to the many watches I have had. You know the kind: "This will do; when it breaks down I'll just get another, they're cheap enough." And so I've had a series of "good-enough" watches. And enough experience to know what I want in a watch. But I put off getting a good one. It seemed that there would be some magical time when I deserved it, or could afford it, or was old enough to get a good one.

So what happened was that I was given some Christmas money and instructed to get something for myself. And I saw a *good* watch at a good price due to the after-Christmas sales. I did an impulsive thing. I bought myself a *good* watch. I walked out wearing it. It even felt good. I went home and had some moments of self-doubt: "I really can't afford this, even on sale." "I really should be paying the Christmas bills with this money." "I don't need a *good* watch."

I took the watch back, expecting to feel good about myself for doing the right thing. But I didn't realize how much I'd miss "my" watch. I remembered that I could see what time it was in the middle of the night because it had a luminous dial, a feature I'd always wanted. I remembered how it fit my wrist perfectly. I remembered how it showed the day and date, all features I'd wanted in a watch all my life. I began to imagine someone else coming along and finding "my" watch at such an incredible price.

I called the jewelry store and told them to hold on to "my" watch because I was coming back to get it. I got a lot of teasing when I got back there the next day. I pleaded temporary insanity. But as I left the store, glad to have "my" watch back again, I thought about the complications I'd just been through. It seems that at this stage even the most trivial things are complicated and paradoxical.

I found myself buffeted between two equal forces: the force of selflessness and continual doing-without, and the force of "isn't it about time you indulged just a little?"

It seems like I've spent far too many precious moments of my middle years being squeezed between the two or more sides of one paradox or another. I'm glad I ended this one. I'm glad they didn't sell my watch. And I'm very happy with it.

And as soon as I get new contact lenses to give me bifocal vision, I just may be able to read my new watch.

(The moral of the story: Life is uncertain. Buy yourself a good watch while you're young enough to read the dial.)

Oh well, so I can't read the date and day on my watch. So I should've gotten a watch like that much earlier in my life so I could have read it for at least a few years. So I strain and strain to read it and finally ask strangers to tell me the date. When it comes right down to it, none of that really matters, because, of course, we all know we can't take any of our material possessions with us. And we certainly didn't bring any with us . . .

### PURE SOURCE

I came
from the pure source,
bearing nothing
but intelligence,

Trusting that
I'd be enfolded and protected
throughout my earthly experience.

And forgetting the pure source,
And learning to protect myself
with things, dependencies and defenses,
I became burdened and slowed,
meandering.

Now I am shedding my accumulations,
seeing how much is not needed
and how much is a hindrance.

Along the way
I shed these things
a bit at a time
like cast-off luggage
and luxuries
along a pioneer trail.

The more I shed
The more I see my way
Back to the pure source.

—❖—

Speaking of accumulations—when we're expecting our first child we expect an eight-pound bundle of joy. We don't foresee the eighty-eight pounds of equipment we must schlep along too. Nor do we foresee the hard work ahead. There's the automatic changing of sheets and blankets while groggy with semi-sleep; the carrying of an infant on one hip and a toddler with an "owie" on the other, crying in three part harmony while stirring the lentils; or the running down the street to collect the naked child who decided to take a stroll at 6:00 A.M. after removing that pesky damp diaper (deposited on the front porch on the way out). I would've never comprehended the concept of "baby fever" at that period. But because I did manage to find a few moments to burrow into the folds of a giggling infant's neck and to do "raspberries" on toddler tummies, I have collected a few memories to fuel the fiery symptoms of a fever that most commonly strikes those whose biological clocks are winding down . . .

## Baby Fever

Baby fever is a little-mentioned ailment that mothers are familiar with. It's not an illness of infancy, however. It affects women in and beyond the childbearing years. It must be contagious, because sometimes husbands succumb too.

Although it is occasionally seen in women who have never had a child, it most often strikes those who have. It never occurs in parents who have an infant and are groggy from changing the diaper, the crib sheets, and the jammies at 3:00 A.M. that morning. It is this very activity that creates natural immunity.

Those who are most at risk for baby fever are those whose babies are no longer babies—those who have blissfully forgotten all about swollen feet, labor and transition, mastitis, diapers, infant wails at 2:00 A.M., car seats and strollers.

The early symptoms include turning into mush when seeing the dimpled fingers of a baby. Baby fever is fully developed in the patient when she, normally competent and composed, begins to launch into gooey baby talk at the sight of an infant, any infant, any place. When the patient begins to do things like examine toes and sniff at the back of the infant's neck, it is time for treatment.

This phenomenon can be explained thusly. The patient has usually had some experience with infants of her own. Perhaps there were several infants. The patient was busy with said infants, busy to exhaustion. So busy that she was almost deprived of full enjoyment of this stage. She was probably up to her cerebellum in diapers. She did her best to enjoy those dimples and coos, but it all went by like a flash, and now it seems like a dream.

Hence, she enters another stage. She romanticizes babyhood. She has forgotten her exhaustion and the demands upon her body. She only remembers the fuzzy little heads and the dimpled hands that patted her.

Now she can spot a baby a hundred yards away in a crowded mall. She is in ecstasy at a passing sniff of "baby musk." She looks at her teenagers and wishes she could turn each of them, one at a time, just for a day, into the babies they were.

But those kids will never be babies again. They march on. They go through adolescence with its constant surprises, acting as if they must do all in their power to repel their mother's love in order to prove that it exists. Not only were babies cuter, they didn't have to do stuff like alter their appearance or defy their teachers.

So she goes on, watching her kids grow up and away. Then a new idea comes into her head. Grandchildren. Perhaps, if she's lucky, she and her kids will survive adolescence and then, lo and behold, perhaps the possibility of grandchildren will appear, like a bright, shining star on the horizon.

Acceptance is the next stage of adapting to baby fever. *Yes,* the patient thinks, *I may not be able to produce my own infant, and why would I want to at this stage—but I can look forward to my own little grandchildren.*

And so she waits patiently, subtly guiding. She is in an infantless limbo. But she is already considering the things she will give her grandchildren. She hopes her children won't think she is too old to baby-sit for them. She works out. She hopes they don't think she is too strange or eccentric. She sends kind, supportive notes to her young adults. She hopes they don't marry and move to the other side of the country. She encourages her husband to consider a recreational vehicle in their future.

But none of these things can fully calm the torment of full-blown baby fever. While there is no full and complete cure for the ailment, there is temporary relief. If you suffer from baby fever, this is what must be done. Offer your services as a baby-sitter to every parent of an infant that you know. Include parents of toddlers. Bring babies into your home when your husband is available if he is also experiencing symptoms.

Baby-sitting will do much to help bring things into perspective. While you will thrill and delight to the chubby cheeks and dimpled knees, you will also remember the hard work. When the baby goes home, its chubby little hand firmly gripping its mother's blouse, you will realize that you are getting too old to do this kind of thing twenty-four hours a day. This will help prevent any crazy ideas. Baby-sitting will also prepare you for your next parenting role, that of grandparenting. And it will give you a chance to hold infants and take in their "baby musk" without making a big commitment. And it will be fun. Since you won't be thinking of the stack of diapers and crib sheets that is waiting for you, you will be able to enjoy the wonder of an infant.

And you may make a little extra money to save towards that RV, just in case you need it later on.

It's ironic that when our kids are babies we look forward to the time when they can go to the cupboard and forage for themselves. And when they are teens, systematically munching their way through anything the least bit edible in the house, then leaving to consume french fries and burritos somewhere else, we reminisce fondly upon the day when we could sit them in a high chair and feed them strained carrots a spoonful at a time. The weeds are always browner on our side of the fence, it seems . . .

# *Wishcraft*

I live near the ocean. There are many who would like to say the same. But many times I wish to live in a pine forest with a view of a craggy peak. I live on a flat surface at sea level. There are times when I wish I could climb in a high altitude.

If I got my wish and were writing this at seven thousand feet surrounded by the scent of the evergreens, I might find myself confessing that there are times when I wish for sea spray, dolphins, and warm sand between my toes.

Sometimes I wish my children were still dimple-fingered, innocent cherubs. When they were, I sometimes wished they were much older.

I have had the experience of wishing for a particular object. I have experienced the anticipation of saving for or juggling income to fulfill such wishes. I have experienced the UPS man coming with the much-awaited package, or the sounds of the cash register formalizing my ownership of the long-anticipated object. In every case, the thrill of the wish fades and the reality never seems to be quite what it was expected to be.

I'm not saying that we should do away with wishful thinking. I'm just wondering if maybe while we're wishing we might not want to also take a look at what we have and where we are. There are some things in the real present for which we can be grateful.

And while we're busy being grateful, there is one other thing we might want to consider about wishes. Having wishes is a much better state than having them all fulfilled and finding there is nothing left to wish for.

Wishing may be an elusive art and at times a mirage on the horizon, but then, how often do we actually see things clearly inside and out? Throughout my thirties I struggled with the dilemma of always having far too much to do. I always thought it was the voices of others that were tormenting me, and I fantasized melting the telephone in the microwave. But as I have continued on this path I have been suspecting that there may be a particular voice that is louder than the others . . .

SCRAP OF PAPER NEXT TO MY BED

Don't touch me, Don't touch me
Don't touch me, don't . . .
Don't ring my phone or
face my door.

Sometimes there are just
too many voices,
like scribbling in the air
blocking out the sun.
And then in the silence
I realize that most
of the voices
are my own.

The many voices in our heads can scribble out the sun and then we can't see very clearly. Sometimes a clear, calm "seeing" is necessary . . .

## *A Fable*

There was a woman who had several children, but none was more of a handful than her firstborn son. From the moment of his birth she was busy with him. He threw his first temper tantrum when he was three weeks old, and learned to remove his diaper and shred it when he was five months old.

When he was old enough to be disobedient, he was. At a very early age he learned to tune his mother out and do his own thing. "My!" she was often heard to say. "Parenting is much more challenging than I had imagined." And other parents would nod in empathy. She assumed that meant they were experiencing the same things.

She would use the same parenting habits with the younger children, and they'd react, "Gee, Mom. You don't have to yell; I heard you." With her firstborn she had learned that she practically had to stand on her head to get his attention. As a result, she had to learn to turn down the volume with his siblings.

When he got to his teens he was even more rebellious than she could've imagined. It didn't matter how many of his belongings she confiscated or how many privileges she removed; he remained disobedient. She took parenting classes, read books, tried reward systems, offered tough love, considered abruptly disowning him; nothing worked.

As time passed she began to realize that he was definitely choosing a lifestyle that she hadn't taught him. And she realized that her other many children were a great deal less disobedient. As the younger ones continued to grow, she became more and more aware of what was the usual and expected rebellion and what was something much stronger. She found that she could work with the younger siblings, to the extent that youngsters are workable. She began to realize that it wasn't necessarily something she had done to cause the first one to run so rapidly off, away from all the values she held dear.

And there was one other thing she was finding it necessary to realize. She needed to realize that this son had his free agency, and he had a right to choose his lifestyle. She had taught him all she could. Now he must choose.

With that realization, and a bit more time, it occurred to her that she'd need to accept the fact that he might end up lost. She had to face that this son she had given birth to might not be hers forever.

When she looked that realization in the face, and shuddered, mourned, and accepted the reality of it, she grew quiet for about a week. Then something unusual began to happen. When she'd see him, she'd really look at him. She figured the time she'd have with him would be very, very short, so she'd really look at him. It was as if her heart was saying, "This will be temporary, so let me memorize him for the future, when I will no longer see him."

Pretty soon she was so busy looking at him she no longer had time to nag him or tell him what he was doing wrong, or to tell him how disappointed she was in him. She was just looking at him.

He'd come into her vision and she'd look. She'd also remember his babyhood and childhood and the good times they'd had before his disobedience had become such an all-consuming issue. He didn't seem to notice her looking and her quiet. But he seemed just a tiny bit more cooperative.

Pretty soon it got so that when she'd be looking she'd be seeing things she hadn't noticed before. Sometimes she'd see pain in his eyes and wonder what it was about. Sometimes she'd see him look at a younger sibling with tenderness. Sometimes she'd see anger or distrust. Sometimes she'd see a blankness, as if he'd given up on life altogether.

It made her sad to be seeing all she saw. She didn't know what to do for this child, so late in his childhood. He seemed to be missing the parenting he'd so adamantly pushed away all his life. And she knew he wouldn't accept any now, so she just continued with her plan to watch him and soak up an eternity with him for the time when he'd be gone.

She became so involved in simply experiencing him that she didn't notice how much he'd calmed down under her watchful eye. And she couldn't read his mind, so she didn't know what he thought one night. He was on his way to the house of a friend who was offering him the right dosage to allow him permanent relief from pain. He'd planned it months before, but as he drove he began to feel confused. The closer he got, the more unsettled he felt, until he finally stopped the car. He closed his eyes and saw in his mind his mother watching him. He examined the vision of her behind his closed eyes. What was it? He looked closely and sank in his seat. It was love, he realized. She was loving him. Not saying a word, just loving him.

He turned his car around, toward home. It wouldn't be easy, he knew. But the path he was on led nowhere. Nowhere at all. What could he lose by trying another?

# PART TWO

———— ❖ ————

# You Can't Live With 'Em . . . and You Can't Shoot 'Em!

*(The Self Versus Another)*

M iddle age means being in the middle of all kinds of relationships. When we were young our primary relationships were with our parents, siblings, and grandparents. That should have forewarned and forearmed us for what was to come: relationships galore. There are the parents to continue to deal with in an ever-evolving universe as they experience new things like aging, illness, and deaths of many loved ones, while continuing to attempt to parent us as we begin to parent them. We still interact with siblings, but now, instead of slug-fests, we try to figure out what went on and we discover that we each had a different childhood. There are also the in-laws, cousins, nieces, nephews, neighbors (and there will always be one or two who will never like the way your grass is cut or the way your children play), coworkers (the sibling replacements?), bosses (parental figures?), teachers, and the person with whom we are assigned to produce the ward newsletter, the one person with whom we'd be the least likely to get along.

Middle age also means that our children will be experiencing their rites of passage, at a time when we are emerging, too, in a much quieter way. We will find ourselves planning weddings while having hot flashes.

Being a teenager was rough. Being a parent of teenagers is worse. Being a parent of teenagers while experiencing middle age is some kind of practical joke.

It cannot be argued that one of the inevitabilities of middle age is teenagers (unless you had your children very early . . .

which, I've been thinking lately, might not have been such a bad idea). Teenagers are talented at keeping entire households in a constant state of amplified angst. Take, for instance, the weeks and hours prior to my son's departure for youth conference . . .

## *Glow*

"No, I'm not going."
"It costs too much."
"I don't care whether I go or not."
"I don't know."
"I suppose."
These are the decisive comments of our son in the weeks prior to youth conference at BYU.

"I need more shorts."
"I need more jeans."
"I need a jacket."
"I could use some shampoo."
These are the sounds of preparation and readiness.

"I'll pack tomorrow."
"I'll pack later."
"I'll pack tonight."
"I'll pack in the morning."
The comments that occurred in the last twenty-four hours before departure time.

"I need to run down to Radio Shack and get batteries!"
"I need to wash these shorts!"
"How come we're out of hair spray?"
"Where's my skateboard?"
These are the excited exclamations at three minutes to departure time. Then off he went in a caravan of four busfuls of spirited stake youth.

It was quieter than usual at home. The brothers he left behind fought 45 percent fewer battles. We wondered how he was doing. Was he just getting by? Was he hanging on the fringes? Was he terrorizing the campus on his skateboard?

Was there any sense in hoping that he might, perhaps, be involved, learning, growing?

The moment I saw him step off the bus I knew the answer to all the questions we had had. He was involved, he learned, he grew.

The youth were transformed. They hugged each other; they glowed with love and strengthened testimonies. It was worth the cost, the uncertainties, the last minute stress, and the new jeans.

And now that he lives apart from us, living his own choices, making his own mistakes, we find some comfort in knowing that there was at least one time in his life when he knew the truth and glowed from that certainty. I pray it will guide him like a distant star in the darkness.

As if it weren't enough that our teens have us in a state of angst, there are plenty of other relationships to do the same. All of our relationships have the potential to be stormy at times . . .

### AFTER THE STORM

The storm built
from ominous gray
to dark, thrashing violence.
Strong words
buffeting my heart,
wondering if I'd survive
and if I did,
what would become of me.
Tears falling in
seemingly endless torrents
washing away
the dust of
vague, unnamed despair
exposing the reality beneath.

This morning
the sky peeks tentatively
through white, pure
puffs of playful clouds.

The sky, a pale aqua
like the hopeful eyes of
the newly born
or the pale eyes
of the elderly
who've sorted memories
and kept only the best ones.


Speaking of memories . . .


## *Yearbooks*

For whatever reason, my twelve-year-old son and nine-year-old daughter have become fascinated by the high school yearbooks of their parents. And it's not as if we leave them lying around the house. They really had to dig for the old books in some musty corner of the garage. I'd pretty much forgotten all about them.

They've been in various rooms of the house for weeks now, depending on who is studying them the most at the moment. My memories of high school are not that pleasant. It wasn't that I was a poor student (I wasn't), and it wasn't that the classes were hard (they weren't. Well, okay, algebra was hard). It's that I was an introvert in a highly sociable setting. These future USC graduates were into cheerleading, cars, fraternities, football, and homecoming. I was into art, poetry, and contemplating the universe. Okay, the Beatles too.

So here are my youngest two kids, examining a past life of mine with a scrutiny that has taken me totally by surprise:

"Was that a friend?"

"You were pretty."

"You had lots of friends."

"You had long hair."

I only half listened to and half responded to their questions and comments. I figured that the fascination would soon pass and the yearbooks could be returned to their musty corner to be forgotten once again.

But not only did the fascination continue, it seemed to increase in intensity (or maybe it was just that I had an overwhelming desire to get on with my life).

The questions became more pointed:

"Was this your boyfriend? How many boyfriends did you have?"

"What was your GPA?"

"Why is this person's picture circled?"

"Why did this person write, 'Did we have fun in Santa Barbara or what?' "

Huh? They were reading the inscriptions in my senior yearbook! Well, if they were going to read those, I better check them out. They might misunderstand some of the inscriptions . . . you know how high school seniors are.

We ended up sitting down together to read them. Most of them were superficial ("Stay as cute and as nice as you are!" "To the girl with the greatest hair!" "Have fun this summer!"), so not much needed to be said. But I was a bit put off when my kids said, "How come so many people said you had great hair?" What is on my head now? Chopped liver?

Some were mysterious. "Who was that, Mom?" "I really don't remember . . . that was a lo-o-o-ng time ago." Some were incriminating. "Really, kids, do you think your mom was that wild? People just like to write stuff like that in yearbooks because they know our kids will read them later."

I still don't understand their fascination. Perhaps it's because they will soon enter adolescence themselves and they are looking for information.

All I know is that after one night of close scrutiny under the direction of my daughter and her countless calm and varied questions, I left the room, ready for bed, and feeling something I'd never felt before. I felt as if I was between two generations who regard me with love (and curiosity). For the first time, I felt surrounded—my parents on one side, my children on the other. Up until that moment I had been feeling that it all flows one way: from parent to child. All that responsibility flowing ever downward.

I figured it was simply my turn to give. But having my daughter examine my life as it existed prior to her birth gave me the strangest feeling—as if we were all equals, not aligned upon some structural hierarchy, but brothers and sisters. It's just that some of us got here earlier.

And her comments upon reading the inscriptions—"You had lots of friends, Mommy"—gave me something I hadn't expected. I realized that while I was remembering that time as all awkward trial and error, growth and stumbling, she readily saw the good that was there, that I was overlooking.

I came away feeling anchored on some kind of solid foundation of love and connection. It wasn't so long ago that I was where she is, just some breaths ago. A few more breaths and she'll be where I am now.

Yearbooks should come with one more inscription: "You won't believe this now . . . but when your kids dig up this yearbook twenty-five years or so later, they will give you an unexpected gift of self-acceptance and love. I know, you don't believe it. Watch; you'll see."

Perhaps all that focus on the yearbooks made my kids more aware of the fleeting moments and gave them a desire to preserve them. Or it could be that they just see too much television.

Christopher, while hugging the dog and talking sweet talk to her, says to me:

"Mom, do you have any Kodak film?"

"Yes, I think so, why?"

"Because this is a Kodak moment!"

A thread connects us, always, no matter what. A bittersweet thread . . .

UMBILICUS

A thread of pain,
an umbilicus
connecting her to me,
me to you.

There is no way
to avoid the pain.
It comes with
the giving of life.

If I could've birthed you
in a joyful instant
instead of hours of
fearful pain,
I would have.

If I could've raised you
through endless sunny days
with no tears, hurts,
disappointments,
I would have.

I look back
and feel sorrow
that I couldn't have
given you perfect love
to fortify you
as you turn your back on me
to face the world.

But I didn't have perfect love
because she didn't either
and so I did the best I could,
as did she.

And I'm sorry
I couldn't love you more.
But I rejoice that
I loved you with a love so fierce
it tore my heart.

It's all I had.
I hope it's enough
for you to mold
into a shape
to give to yours.

We take what we have and mold it into something that is useful in our present situation. When we are younger we may not have as much as we'll have when a few years have taught us some lessons . . .

# "Grand"-Parenting

My first two children were born when I was in my mid- to late twenties, my last two in my early and mid-thirties.

I have noticed some differences in how I have parented the early children and the "cabooses." I was definitely more of a raging type-A mom with those unfortunate first two.

I've been more of a mellow parent with the second two, mellow yet without letting them get away with anything. Actually it has been easier to be firm and consistent with the youngest two because I haven't been tied down with babies like I was with the first two. The second two know that I can come after them.

So, the first ones had a strict, raging mom who ruled from the rocking chair. They will probably tell their therapists all about it.

But all of that is water under the bridge now. They are now ranging from preteen to young adult in years, and I seem to be right on schedule too. From a biological standpoint I am old enough to be a grandparent, and I seem to be acting more and more like one with my kids.

I don't know what it is. I don't know if it's a hormonal thing or an emotional thing. Perhaps because I am at the midpoint of my life I am subconsciously aware of my own mortality. Or maybe I'm just tired.

Let me illustrate:

It was a school holiday, and I was attempting to take a shower while the kids were in other rooms planning and implementing devious activities to give me extra work to do. I took the cordless phone into the bathroom with me so that they could page me if there were any emergencies. This method is one of the only ways I can ensure some privacy for a few moments when they are all home. Otherwise they'd be coming into the bathroom every three seconds.

After I stepped out of the shower (I've managed somehow to train them to postpone emergencies until after they hear the shower turn off), I heard the phone beeping. I picked it up, and my daughter, age nine, was telling me all about a sandwich she'd made and "Can we have some cookies,

Christopher says we're all out of cookies, that's not true, is it? When are you going to come out? My tooth is loose, I can feel it when Ah fay thith, see? And Christopher stabbed me with a spoon."

In the past I probably would've said, "There are cookies, I'll get you some when I come out [they're hidden]; listen, I will be out in a minute, okay? How do you guys expect me to get dried off if you keep paging me? We can talk about these things when I come out!"

But it was different this time. Instead of being irritated, I was amused. There was something about the quality of my daughter's voice that struck me. Here was this young voice (sounding even younger over the telephone) so eager and trusting, pouring out her experiences in process, complete with muffled sounds as her tongue explored her loose tooth. Even the part about being stabbed with a spoon amused me (its being a blunt, rounded object helped some). I felt that this was a temporary thing that would soon be gone, and I'd better enjoy it while I had it.

So instead of speaking to her with irritation, I was surprised to find myself, dripping wet, actually enjoying our conversation. "You do, huh? . . . He did, huh?" She responded with "Yeah." That was all.

After the tooth came out, she came to me at my desk to show me the vacancy left by that tooth, the new molar growing in on another side, and something else having to do with her teeth; I didn't catch it because she was not speaking very clearly once again. She had pulled her mouth out on both sides so I could get a good look. I watched this and almost said, "Okay, I'll examine the interior of your mouth at bedtime. Right now I need to finish typing this." But I didn't do that.

Instead, I watched with every cell of my body and soul. I wished for a video camera built into my eye. She looked so funny with her mouth pulled so wide, and she was being so serious about it all.

My seventeen-year-old left me a note this morning. I found it at 5:50 A.M. It said:

Mom:

Since I went to bed at 9:30, and no one reminded me (to my knowledge) of KP [it was his night to do dishes], I had this feeling in the back of my head that I had forgotten something. At 10:00 P.M. I realized that I hadn't done KP. So I did it. If it's absolutely imperative that I go to seminary then get me up. If not please let me sleep so I won't fall and hurt myself while going to school since I'm so tired. Thank you.

> Love,
> (illegible signature)

At the bottom was a cartoon of a yawning character and a part bird/part airplane.

A few years ago I would've seen this as a bunch of lousy excuses, and I would've lectured my son on how we didn't need to remind him it was his night to do the dishes, there is a chart on the wall, et cetera.

This time, however, I was amused, even at 5:00 A.M. I thought the note was something to keep.

Now, there is nothing particularly clever or special about the note, or about my daughter's tooth explanations. And there isn't anything especially memorable about my twelve-year-old's struggles to do his math homework, or about the way he is always trying to get a hug.

These are ordinary events and ordinary days. Maybe that's what it is that makes me so appreciate them.

Having a child who is a young adult, maybe I have become aware of how temporary this childful time is. Maybe I have realized that all too soon there will be no more loose teeth and no more stabbings with spoons. The grandchildren will be carrying these traditions on, but it will all be second-hand to me. Now is when I am in it.

So, there is something to be said for child-rearing over forty. I may not have the stamina of a twenty-year-old . . . but I have the appreciation of a grandmother.

——❖——

Sometimes it takes more than the perspective of years to better appreciate things. Sometimes we may need to be knocked out of our orbits of routine by something that makes us stop and take notice. Just ask Karen . . .

## *Karen*

A friend didn't actually tell me this story, but let's suppose one did. It could have happened. And if it did happen, my friend might tell it like this:

"I had a friend named Karen who was very nice. She was well liked everywhere but in her own neighborhood. It seemed to be because of the fact that she had three boys who were about as normal as boys can be, meaning that they sometimes stepped in flower beds or made sudden, annoying noises. It could also be because Karen was a single parent. Being both Mom and Dad stretched Karen pretty far, so she sometimes wasn't outside to warn a boy about the flower bed he was about to step into because she was busy grating the cheese for the macaroni.

"I could accept the fact that an irritable neighbor might occasionally feel resentment toward Karen. I believe it was true that two of her boys climbed on the roof at 6:00 A.M. one Saturday morning while Karen and one of the boys were still sleeping. Karen had been up until 3:00 A.M. with the now-sleeping boy, getting him through the stomach flu which his brothers had the week before and Karen would probably have the next week. So, in her sleepy state, she hadn't realized at first that two of her boys were on the roof making Tarzan and ape noises, which woke up several neighbors before they woke up Karen.

"Once she was awake, you can be sure she brought those boys inside and let them know exactly how she felt about that kind of behavior. But one might say it was only natural that Karen would be the target of annoyance in the neighborhood. Karen herself would agree that that would be a possibility. She often found herself apologizing to her neighbors.

"But it went beyond mere annoyance. At first it was just that, but as time went on it went from annoyance to irritation. Then from irritation to resentment. After resentment it became an out-of-control monster. Karen and her boys became the neighborhood scapegoats. If a lawn was littered with soda cans, it was automatically assumed to be the doings of Karen's boys. If anyone received a funny phone call, it was Karen's boys. If a tree branch were to break off . . . Karen's boys. It got to the point where Karen's boys were blamed for anything that went awry in the neighborhood, even while they were spending two weeks at their grandmother's house, as if they had the power to create chaos from three hundred miles away. I wouldn't have been surprised if I'd heard a neighbor blame the water rate hike on Karen's boys.

"Karen was aware of what was happening. And she knew it wasn't right. She felt powerless to change it. There were a few times when her boys were blamed for something and she knew it wasn't them, because it was one of those nights when she had them each seated in three corners of the kitchen so she could eat her dinner in peace. On nights like that they sat with their faces to their corners, ate late, and went to bed early. And Karen sat in their room paying bills until they fell into a deep sleep, their mouths open and their arms dangling. She sometimes looked forward to evenings like that. She knew where they were and what they were doing. The next morning, when a neighbor complained that his trash cans had been knocked over the evening before, Karen knew for a fact that it wasn't her boys.

"The assuming and the blaming were enough to handle, but as time went on Karen found herself more and more excluded. The neighbors no longer asked to borrow a cup of sugar or an egg. No one asked her to collect their mail. No one brought over cookies or surplus zucchini. Karen began to realize that no one in the neighborhood was talking to her.

" 'Now, isn't that sad,' Karen sighed. It went on for some time and spread like a disease. Soon rumors began to circulate to justify the treatment of Karen. When new neighbors moved in, they were warned to watch out for Karen and her wild boys.

"Away from home Karen moved among a circle of friends, peers, and associates. Back on her street she was confined to the role of the neighborhood scapegoat. It began to cause her some sorrow.

"About then I had a wicked idea. It was something I would've never considered before. But I couldn't stand to watch all those people throwing stones at Karen. It had to stop, and my idea was the best I could come up with. I had to take a chance. So I wrote a letter anonymously to each of Karen's neighbors. It said:

Dear neighbor:

Karen doesn't talk about this and would probably rather not, but she is dying. She spends her quiet moments in bed at night trying to figure out how to find a balance between meeting her obligations and finding meaning in her life. She realizes fully how short her life will be. She must also give some priority to doing those things that will prolong her life a little bit. Her life will be much too short. And then she will die. What can you do to ease her burdens, find meaning, and brighten what time she has left for her life?

A friend

"Perhaps it's not really so wicked. Everything I said in the letter was true. Sure, Karen wasn't diagnosed with a terminal illness. I never said she was, and besides, *life* is terminal. And I knew that like all of us, Karen struggled to lead a meaningful, if fleeting, life. So I was simply telling the truth.

"Well, when those letters went out there was quite a stir. Karen didn't know about the letters, but it didn't take her long to become curious. Something was up. First the neighbors were tearful, clutching each other, weeping, moaning, carrying on, and generally being extremely dramatic. It was as if this was just what they were waiting for: a tragedy to react to. They'd probably seen too many soap operas. Karen would peek out her window to see them collected into little groups, talking with great intensity, their faces distorted, turning periodically toward Karen's house. She wondered what that was all about. But when it was time to go to work she'd forget all about it.

"But the events that soon followed made her even more curious. The neighbors were being overly nice to Karen. When she'd pass them they'd wave and smile broadly. When Mr. Henry asked her how her boys were doing Karen began to get suspicious. 'Oh, you know them, Mr. Henry. There's always *something* for them to get into.'

" 'Well,' Mr. Henry smiled, 'boys will be boys.' It wasn't just his words that startled Karen, it was his face. When he said the second 'boys' his face seemed to cloud up, almost as if he might cry; then he looked away.

" 'Something fishy is going on around here,' Karen said aloud to her boys as they went inside.

" 'Yeah,' her middle son said, 'Mrs. Rogers was nice to me today. She said, "That's okay," when I fell on her new flower pot while I was catching the Frisbee. Maybe she's happy because she made a deal with the gypsies. She used to tell me she was going to sell me to them!'

"The next day Mrs. Rogers brought over a huge batch of snickerdoodles. 'I'm sure your boys love homemade cookies,' she said. 'And you surely don't have time to bake.' She smiled and stroked the hair of the youngest son, even though he was particularly dirty.

"And on the same day Margaret came over and said, 'You know, your boys truly must be a handful; is there anything I can do to relieve you of your tremendous burdens?' When Margaret said that, Karen had to sit down. After all the complaints and rumors it sounded very strange. And when Karen added Margaret's words to the cookies and Mr. Henry's strange behavior, she became convinced that there was something behind all this sudden benevolence.

" 'What's up, Margaret?' she asked.

" 'Wh-what do you mean?' Margaret stuttered.

" 'Suddenly everyone is being sickeningly sweet to us. Something's up.'

" 'Well . . . uh . . .' Margaret looked around furtively.

"Karen sensed that if she would ever get to the bottom of this, it would have to be through Margaret. Margaret was more of a follower than the others. Karen pushed on, and it wasn't long before Margaret produced her copy of my letter. When Karen read it she instantly understood its intent and its meaning and she burst out laughing.

"Margaret was uneasy. She wasn't sure what the laughter meant. 'Is it . . . is it . . . *true?*' she asked.

" 'Of course it's true,' Karen said.

" 'Y-you're really going to die?'

" 'Yes, of course,' Karen said matter-of-factly. 'And life is much too short for petty resentments, isn't it?' Margaret just stared, admiring Karen's courage.

"Karen never did tell her neighbors that her death, as far as she could hope, would come after a long, full life. Why should she tell her neighbors that? Wasn't that when most of us hoped to die? If assuming that her death was imminent caused her neighbors to be more kind and thoughtful to everyone, why should she meddle?

"And I never told her I wrote the letter. But I did notice she had a special smile for me whenever she saw me. And I thought I saw her wink at me once."

Karen's neighbors let down their barriers of resentment. But those barriers can come up when we least expect them to, or when we need others the most . . .

SAFETY'S COST

We bump into each other's
rough edges and withdraw
in pain,
intensified by
a sense of betrayal.

We pull in and
build a case
to mistrust
and justify it
with our murmurings.

We surround ourselves
with a cushion of
silence. . . .

There, we're safe
and sad.

Do we ever let in
the possibility,
hasn't it been declared?
that harm is not intended
toward us?

It only seems that it is
through the distorting
layers of our own fortress
built to protect
and isolate.

Sometimes the isolating barrier we erect about us is to preserve our dignity. Somewhere along the path toward middle age we learned that someone, somewhere, might find it unseemly if we were to break out in a moment of spontaneous play. Or maybe it's because we tend to become heavily laden with all our must-do's. Whatever the case, we must all remember to take a moment to stop and pop the bubble wrap . . .

## Bubble Wrap

Being at an age when I can no longer hedge about whether I am a grown-up (no matter how grown-up—or un-grown-up—I feel, my age indicates that I am grown-up, and in fact have been for quite some time), it is plausible to make a contrast between grown-ups (as in myself) and children (as in those many energetic beings who surround me daily).

For instance:

• When my daughter finds two quarters in her wallet, she feels instantly rich and begins to imagine the wonders that those two coins will provide for her. She fantasizes about bubble gum and sodas and popcorn, and she beams and prances about.

When I find two quarters in my wallet, I know I am broke.

• When my son's hair doesn't turn out the way he wants it to, it is a major, global crisis. The United Nations will hear about it.

When my hair doesn't turn out the way I want it to, I am definitely not surprised, and I simply add it to my long list of daily humiliations and get away from the bathroom mirror ASAP, muttering something about being grateful that at least I have hair.

• When my children have about fifteen extra minutes of homework, they come home and rant and rave about how difficult school is, how they are overwhelmed with work to do, how they can't possibly get everything done, how stressed they are . . . and then they plop down with a computer catalog and an apple or run outside to play.

When my children come home with their tales of childhood burnout and overload, I listen semi-patiently and then go see if the laundry pile has gotten down to ten feet yet; count how many telephone messages I need to return; sort the messages into three piles: "Urgent" (medical test results, teachers, financial matters, etc.), "ASAP" (church responsibilities, friends and relatives, etc.), and "It Ain't Gonna Happen" (bake sales, paper drives, Tupperware parties, encyclopedia salesmen, etc.); and begin to wash and cut up forty potatoes for dinner.

• When my children see a freshly raked pile of leaves, their legs begin to twitch and they think of jumping and playing.

When I see a freshly raked pile of leaves, I think of blisters.

• When my son brings home a new box of Legos, he imagines towering structures and innovative vehicles.

I imagine how the little pieces will look spread over our carpets.

• Give a kid a donut and he's in heaven.

Give an adult a donut and he's in the other place as he assesses the fat content of the item and what it might do to his cholesterol. And if he gives in to the temptation, there is no enjoyment, as guilt shuts down his sense of taste.

• If there is a lot of mud, kids think of a lot of fun.
Adults think of a lot of mess . . . a whole lot.

• If a package comes to me wrapped in bubble wrap, my
kids will pounce on it and spend an entire ten minutes pop-
ping the little bubbles and find it extremely satisfying.

If the package comes when no kids are around, I will
carefully store the bubble wrap, glad to know that I'll have it
the next time I need to send a package to someone.

Perhaps it could be said that children have too much fun
and lack a sense of responsibility. And on the other hand,
grown-ups have too little fun and are bent over with responsibility.

Could we maybe compromise? The next time a piece of
furniture is moved into your house, do you suppose you could
think about climbing on it, and could you teach your kids to
think first about what it will be like to dust it?

Okay, so maybe we can't get them to think about things
like dusting right off. Maybe if we're more playful they'll be
more responsible. Maybe if tonight we served them Ding
Dongs for dinner (and for the rest of the week) they may
eventually come around to saying, "Don't you want to feed us
something nutritious or something?"

I suppose they'll learn to be responsible soon enough, perhaps even too soon and too well. But what's happened to us
adults? Must we abandon play? I don't think so. But we may
need to remember how by watching children.

Okay, you guys, the next bubble wrap is mine!


Our children know how to find opportunities to play at
any given moment. But then, we must admit that they also
do some serious thinking . . .


## *Charity*

There is a family in our ward by the name of Harvey.
Their children are roughly the same ages as our children.
There is a daughter in the family by the name of Charity. My
daughter is familiar with the family primarily because there
is another daughter who is her age.

Now that you have been duly introduced to the Harvey family, I can tell you the story. Most nights I collect my two younger children so we can read scriptures together before bed. There were several nights in a row that we were reading scriptures about faith, hope, and charity. (And perhaps you are already seeing where this is leading.) They are among my favorite scriptures, and I thought they were becoming the kids' favorites also. They both looked so thoughtful as I read to them, especially Kiera, who concentrated with furrowed brow. I truly attempted to emphasize the concept of charity as a necessary characteristic.

On the second night there was a scripture about the need to have charity in order to reside in the kingdom of God. I asked them some questions about what we could do to have charity in our family.

Kiera spoke up confidently. "We don't have charity in our family," she stated. I thought, *Well, this is good. Perhaps she has become aware that our family could use a bit more charity. I'm glad she is sensitive to that.* Then she completed her statement: "The Harveys have Charity."

They do, indeed.


The Harveys have Charity . . . so what does that leave us with? Pocket lint!

## *List of Life*

I remember the day I did it. But I can barely recall the quality of the chaos that surrounded me. Some instinct must have caused me to make the list. It was as if I felt compelled to note a time that was about to pass unnoted.

On a simple piece of crumpled paper I'd written a list of everything that was in my pocket after the kids had all left for school one morning. I had begun my day with empty pockets and, no doubt, some trepidation. Two hours later, the kids in school, I must've sighed with relief and put a hand in my pocket to find the evidence of the activities of those two hours.

Here's the list:

1. Ponytail holder (to keep my five-year-old daughter's hair out of her cereal and milk).
2. Wad of hairy gum (cut from eight-year-old son's hair).
3. Cotton ball that smells of nail polish remover (used to remove gum from behind son's ear).
4. Marking pen (used to write names on lunch sacks, books, a teddy bear, and a video of *The Secret Garden*).
5. Permission slip to go on a field trip (remembered and signed at the last minute, and then forgotten anyway).
6. Threads and clothing labels (cut from the backs of clothes that have been washed repeatedly but suddenly the labels are unbearably "scratchy").
7. Hairbrush (self-explanatory).
8. Absence note (written with the wrong child's name and crumpled).
9. Absence note (with correct name, folded neatly and forgotten).
10. Tube of hair gel (self-explanatory).
11. Marbles (collected at the door).
12. Lipstick-stained tissue (from wiping the face of kindergarten daughter).
13. Dog leash (dog attempted to follow kids to school).
14. Overdue library book notice (handed to me casually at the door and then offender ran off to school).
15. Paper towel (used to wipe the milk off kindergartner's mouth at the door).
16. Damp sock (was used for nose blowing and tears wiping by child who cried about someone who always picks on him at school if he wears something "dorky like this").
17. Burnt toothpick (son was lighting pilot lights for me with a toothpick).
18. Dandelion (daughter ran back home to present it to me after finding it on way to school, and then discovered that there was no one to walk back to school with her. I had to get car keys and take her).
19. Car keys (self-explanatory).

Emptying my pockets in the empty house, I might have marveled at what I found. Or maybe it was similar to all the other mornings of that busy time of young children. But something made me write the list. And looking at it now, I'm glad I did. I see that time has moved on, evolving and shaping my day gradually. I hadn't realized that so much had changed.

I don't mean big changes, these are little changes I hardly notice unless I come across something that reminds me. For instance, when did my daughter no longer need for me to pull her hair into a ponytail before she ate her breakfast? When did she learn to keep her hair out of the milk? Was there a day when we said, "This is no longer needed"?

Now the oldest boy lives somewhere else. The second son drives away in his own car, which is difficult to start and vibrates like a washing machine in the spin cycle, but it is his own independence which he has earned for himself. Son number three has more serious concerns today than gum in his hair. And the former kindergartner who smeared lipstick on her face and thought I wouldn't notice is now talking about wanting to get a scholarship to BYU.

Today my pockets are lighter. They tend to be filled with only a stray rubber band, paper clip, or grocery list. My children are becoming increasingly independent. They don't need me to do as much for them.

Now all I have to do is stay up late to have long talks with them; pray continuously for them; worry when they're late coming home; hope that I taught them enough of what they'll need to know; spend time with them so they'll stay connected enough to share their feelings and thoughts; encourage them; guide them; influence them; reason with them; get back up with them over and over again; let go of them when I must, an invisible thread stretching from my hands and heart to wherever they are; cry over their mistakes; be patient with them; hope; pray; stay up all night; be endlessly vigilant. That's all.

Once my pockets were full of the evidence of a full life. Now it is my heart, mind, and soul.


Whether it is our relationships with our children or with others, there is no formula that always works in every situation except maybe one: love one another and express that love . . .

## *Lori*

When her sister, Nancy, married, Lori thought she'd lost her best friend. At the reception her eyes filled with tears, and everyone thought she was swept up in the emotions that the others were feeling.

Lori resented her new brother-in-law. All she seemed to hear from her sister lately was Derek-this and Derek-that. What about all those talks that went on into the night? What about going to get haircuts together and frozen yogurt? What about shopping together? What about all the things Lori borrowed from Nancy and all the things Nancy gave her, like her earrings and advice?

At the reception Lori hardly said a word to Derek. Most of them thought she was just being shy. But Derek didn't think that was it.

Nancy and Derek didn't live very far away, so Lori saw them often. Derek was a graphic artist who worked in an office he set up in the dining room of their apartment, and Nancy worked in a dental office. Lori never went to the apartment when Nancy wasn't there, because, she said, she didn't want to interrupt Derek's work.

But when Lori's mom was in the hospital, Derek told Lori to come on over after her classes were through and he'd take her to visit her mom, then pick up Nancy and they could have dinner together.

The arrangement lasted for two weeks, until Lori's mom came home. But the relationship between Lori and Derek lasted much longer. Derek became the big brother Lori had never had. He listened to her with even more patience than her own father ever could. She looked forward to those times she could spend with Derek and Nancy. She realized that she truly hadn't lost a sister but had gained a brother. She was still the recipient of all her sister had to offer her, but now it was supplemented and enriched by all that her brother-in-law brought.

As a college student she found she had the perfect job to help pay for her books. She baby-sat her nephew on the weekends so that Derek and Nancy could spend some time together. By then her father had passed away, and Derek filled in as both a brother and a father, helping her with tuition and encouraging her to continue with her education.

Lori would sometimes recall the feelings she had had when her sister married Derek, and she realized that her fears were unfounded. She felt especially blessed and looked forward to her own wedding day. She felt confident that she would find someone who would fit in nicely, bringing his own contributions to the family.

But the only thing she hadn't expected happened. Derek was killed in an automobile accident. A car crossed the center line and hit him head-on. He died instantly. Lori knew that this time she needed to give something to her sister. She knew that Nancy needed her to be strong and to offer comfort. But Lori, no matter how much she tried, was unable to strengthen herself enough to give her sister anything.

Lori cried for days and days. How could she be any help to her sister when she was so sad? She knew Nancy needed her. She felt selfish. She could barely get through five minutes without sobbing. She missed Derek so much. What would her life be like without him? How could she say that? He was only her brother-in-law. He was Nancy's husband. How could she be so selfish to mourn so deeply when it was Nancy who had the right to such grief?

At the funeral Lori watched Nancy. She was the strong one. She wasn't falling apart the way Lori did when she saw Nancy hold their baby son up to say good-bye to his father. *I've got to get it together,* Lori thought, *for Nancy.*

After the funeral, Lori dreaded being alone with Nancy. She put it off as long as she could. She felt that if she felt this bad, then Nancy must feel a hundred times worse. And how could she be supportive? She was too weakened by grief.

Finally the time came to sit with Nancy and face her. Lori could hardly bear to look at her. When she did, she saw Nancy's face was full of compassion for her. "You're really taking it hard, aren't you, Lor?"

*What is this?* Lori thought. *You're the one who has lost your husband. Yet you are attempting to comfort me?* Lori resisted, but Nancy's soft words and loving expression broke down her carefully built wall. She began to sob uncontrollably.

Nancy took her into her arms to soothe her, and Lori was embarrassed to find herself blubbering like she'd seen others do and swore she never would.

"I miss him so much, Nancy. How will I fill this aching hole I feel? I can't seem to stop hurting! When will I be able to smile again? I think the sun went down and it hasn't come up again. It hurts so much . . . so much . . . it hurts . . ."

Nancy continued to stroke Lori while her own tears flowed unchecked. "I know, I know, let it all out, come on. . . . Tell me how it hurts."

When Lori had finished and her sobs had quieted she felt as if she was just a little bit lighter. But then she felt embarrassed. Nancy was the widow, not her. How could she have done this? What a weak child she was. She poured out her pain on the one who must be feeling the most pain of all. How could she have done this to her sister? She let Nancy down when she needed her.

Lori stood up and said, "I'm sorry!" And then, unable to bring herself to say another word, she ran home.

All night she thought about it and considered ways to make it up to her sister. *Next time I'm in a situation like this, I'll forget all about my own pain and concentrate on the other person.* She knew that was right; it was the Golden Rule. Then later she thought about how her sister encouraged her to share her pain. *She must be some kind of saint,* Lori thought. But then she remembered sharing a room with her for seventeen years and doubted that.

The next morning a dozen daisies arrived with a letter for Lori, addressed in her sister's hand. She tore into the envelope and read:

Dear Lori,

I want to thank you for helping me. I felt like I was numb or stuck or something. It was as if the pain was so intense that I was paralyzed. Everyone was doing their best to be supportive of me. But I felt like they were all looking at me, and I felt very much alone. It was becoming unbearable, and I didn't quite understand it or know what to do about it.

I didn't figure it out until this morning. It was that I felt like I was alone in my grief. And I felt helpless. Everyone was doing everything for me. I was left to mourn alone while others watched and said, "I'm sorry." What I needed more than anything else was for someone to mourn with me. And I needed to feel like I was still capable of making a contribution of some kind. I can't heal if I can't serve others. And serving others instead of being focused on "poor me" allows me to share another's burden, thereby lessening my own.

You, dear Lori, were there to give me exactly what I needed. Your tears and your words proved to me that I was not mourning alone, that you felt as I did, that you shared my pain and my loss. There was no doubt that you felt the same pain. And you gave me an opportunity to give. I can't tell you how much holding you comforted me.

Thank you,
Nancy

Lori carefully folded the letter. She felt a kind of peace wash over her. She rose to get a drink of water, and as she felt the cool, clear water against her parched lips, she noticed the sun was shining brightly in the yard.

Our relationships with others always seem to be more complex than they appear on the surface. When someone dies there is an empty place around which we must negotiate for years, if not a lifetime . . . a silence that is louder than anything physical. Our pasts intermingle like jigsaw puzzle pieces, and so do our fears . . .

### BLIND SPOT

Who are you? I want to know.
I thought I knew you
Like the inside of my eyelids
With the sun beating against them
Or the familiar skyline of my teeth
As known by my tongue

Years of history, seeing your features
Every day coming in the door,
A comfort? Or an intruder?
A boy, a man, a husband,
A stranger, an imaginary playmate.

I think I might know you
Like the russet-colored hairs
Making a curled fringe about your skin,
Or like I know the shape
And texture of your hands,
Or like I know how your voice
Sounds in the early morning.

But an empty spot
Is sore in my heart.
It's the place where
I can't see the future.
It's the place where
I keep my fears.

When you are in that place
You are a stranger, unrecognizable
And I am a little girl,
Afraid of strangers.

I can play lightly
Around the empty spot
But I cannot deny its existence.


The future is an uncertainty, that's for certain. But sometimes the present is too. Sometimes we are unaware of those around us . . .


## The Room

Steve has recently received his mission call. He'll be going to Canada. It's a long way from his home in New Mexico, and not just in distance.

He's been thinking in bed more than sleeping lately. He's

been thinking about not seeing his family for two years. That seems really strange to him. But then, he also wonders if he really knows them that well.

One night, after the house is quiet, he hears a sound in his room. He sits up and turns on his light, catching his mom standing near the doorway. "Oops," she says quietly.

"What are you doing, Mom?" Steve rubs his eyes.

"Oh, I'm, um, just looking."

"At what?"

"Well, your room, and you."

"Do you often do this?" Steve considers that he may have missed something. He's always been a sound sleeper in the past.

"Well, actually, no, it's just you'll be leaving soon . . ."

"Aw, Mom, I won't be gone long, it'll be okay, I'll miss you too."

"Actually, I was checking to see if my craft table would fit along this wall."

"Oh. I'm not even gone yet!"

"I will miss you, Steven. That's probably why I suddenly felt compelled to come in here and check this wall. I was thinking that it might help if I had something to look forward to. It would be nice to work on my crafts in here instead of in the garage." Steve's mom sits on the bed next to him.

It occurs to Steve that he hasn't paid much attention to what his mom does at her craft table in the garage. He asks her lots of questions, and she explains all about her book covers, many-pocketed aprons, and bean bag pillows. Before she leaves the room she promises to make him a bean bag pillow to take and she'll send him a book cover.

The next morning he sees his mom as if he hadn't really noticed her before.

That night he hears a strange kind of a sliding noise in his room. He turns on the light, and this time he sees his brother, Tim, wielding a metal tape measure.

"Oh, hi," Tim says. "I didn't know you were here."

"And that's why you haven't turned on a light, right?"

"Funny you should put it that way."

"What does *that* mean?"

"I was just thinking—" Tim approaches the bed, and Steve moves over. "This room won't be in use for a couple of years, so I thought I could turn it into a darkroom."

"You better check with Mom. She was measuring it for her craft table. And since when do you develop photos anyway?"

"That's just it. I would've been doing that all this time if I'd had a darkroom." Tim tells Steve all about how frustrated he's been with not being able to have final control over his photographic images and about how he'd probably be a famous photographer someday if he could do that. They talk until one o'clock in the morning. Steve had no idea that Tim was so passionate about photography.

The next night Steve has just fallen into a deep, exhausted sleep, when he hears a bump in his room. He automatically turns on his light and moves over in bed. It's his dad.

"Hi, Dad. What do you want to use my room for?"

"What makes you think I want to use your room?"

"You bumped into my chair, you were measuring with your feet."

"Oh, I guess maybe I was. I really came in to talk to you."

Steve's dad talks about his mission, about how the experience will help Tim prepare for the rest of his life, about how he'll be blessed for his service, et cetera. When he finally runs out of things to say, Steve asks, "Okay. So what do you want to use my room for?"

"I thought I could use it as a music room—you know, shelves for CDs and a nice chair to relax in. Maybe a little piano could go over there." He points to Steve's overflowing laundry basket.

They talk some more about how Steve's dad used to teach a music appreciation class and how much he enjoyed it. That was back in the days when he didn't need a higher paying job to support the family and prepare for missions and college. Steve sees his dad smile with true pleasure as he talks about music. He hadn't realized music was so important to his dad.

The next night Steve waits, listens, and thinks. Sure enough, his door creaks open slowly. He turns on the light and jumps from his bed.

"EEEEEeeeiiiowww!" his sister screams and drops a stack of clean, formerly folded shirts.

"What do you want?" Steve asks.

"I don't want anything! Mom told me to slip these shirts into your room. She said you'd be looking for them in the morning."

"Oh. Thanks."

"That's all you can say? My heart is racing!"

"Sorry. I just thought you were coming to claim my room."

"Why would I be doing that?"

"You don't want my room?"

"No, at least not while you're still in it."

Steve moves over. It's getting to be a routine.

His sister sits and says, "You know, I have wished there was someplace I could go where I could read and write in quiet."

She speaks for some time about how hard it's been since Grandma moved into her room. She loves Grandma and all, but she really craves some solitude. She'd like a place to put bookshelves and a writing desk. She talks about some of the ideas she has for stories she'd like to write.

The next morning Steve hands her a stack of his favorite books. "You can have these while I'm gone," he says. Even she looks different to him now.

He looks at everyone differently. *They all have their own unique qualities and gifts,* he thinks. *Why didn't I notice that before? Why is it that we don't pay attention to anything we feel is permanent, and if it suddenly seems less so we suddenly pay attention?*

Steve decides he'll have to be sure to write often to each of them. And he's really glad that he won't be around when they start to debate the appropriate use of his room.

Wombs, rooms, nothing can contain our rapidly advancing offspring for long, except maybe the families they go on to create . . .

## *Give Peace a Chance*

I've known many moms- and dads-to-be, hovering on the brink of the great unknown. They alternate between a Mona-Lisa-like bliss and great impatience. Pregnancy, they have concluded after eight and one-half months of it, or less, is the pits. Nothing, they've concluded, could be any worse than pregnancy. Not late night feedings, the terrible twos, or sibling rivalry. They've heard all about those things and have decided that pregnancy is worse.

I remember being in the ninth month of my first pregnancy and having a friend, a seasoned mom of three boys, tell me that in spite of how I was feeling I ought to enjoy the last bit of peace I was experiencing, because the day would come when I'd wish I could put 'em back there.

"No," I declared without hesitation, "I'll never want to put one back *here!*" Not only was I sure of it, I was sure of it even after the fourth had been born. But then, they were all still young. Their problems were also young. Then some of them defected. They became teenagers.

When children are young their boo-boos can be healed with a kiss and a Band-Aid featuring Snoopy in sunglasses. And when the noise gets to where it is bouncing off the interior of the parent's skull, there is the blessed peace of naptime. It is almost as good as the peace one could feel while pregnant and imagining pink pea-pod baby toes. And it is the last peace a parent will ever feel in connection with their children while inhabiting earth.

As adolescence comes marching in there is no longer a naptime (unless it is for sleeping in after a very late night), the boo-boos become boom-booms which cannot be simply kissed away, and never again will a parent have much control over where the little darlings are and what they are doing. And that is why peace becomes such an object of nostalgia.

Parents of teenagers:

—Have children who forget to call them to let them know: (a) where they are, (b) that they'll be late, and (c) that they are still alive and well.

—Realize that before, when they heard sirens they were afraid they would wake the baby. Now they inspire another kind of fear.

—Get about the same amount of sleep as parents of newborns, but none of the sympathy.

—Know why their hair is graying.

—Feel that childhood went by too quickly and adulthood is too far off.

—Must learn the lesson that there is actually very little they have control over after all.

—Have to let go and watch their children go stumbling off into the world like giant toddlers who aren't finished yet but who have outgrown their cribs, and with a few mature traits must go out there and fall flat on their faces if they are to develop any more of them.

—Realize that they will always be parents and they will never have any peace again.

—Might actually consider, if it were possible, putting one back—not for a period of peace, but in order to give the child one more round of parenting, because the childhood was too short, the chances to teach were too few, and the world expects so much.

But on second thought, there's always the parent curse: "I hope when you're a parent you have a kid just like you!" That should serve as one more round to smooth out the rough edges.

There may be only a few more summers for us to experience the grand tradition of the family vacation. Only a few more times to make the strong impression that we are a family . . .

## *Paradise*

I have always enjoyed vacationing with my family. There is just something about it that is so appealing to me. But at first I couldn't quite figure out what it was. I mean, if we were all to cram ourselves into one room for a couple of days, simulating a motel room, we'd probably end up with emergency vehicles in our driveway. Put us all in a tent in the backyard to reenact our last camping trip and we'd mutiny.

But there we'd be, all crammed into a car for countless hours, fishing poles poking the backs of our necks, waiting for the next disgusting gas station restroom, and having a great time together. Does this make sense?

Then I analyzed the last trip we took together. I found some reasons for the paradise.

First of all, we're all together in a committed sort of way. I mean, when you're traveling on a highway across the desert at seventy-five mph, you're not likely to say, "I gotta get outta here," and open the door. So perhaps it's true what they say—commitment makes things go more smoothly. Since there is nowhere else to be, and since we're all in each other's faces, perhaps we put forth the effort to get along.

Then there are no schedules other than departure times. I don't have to nag anyone to hurry up or they'll be late for school, or to finish their social studies homework. Our normal schedule is like too tight shoes. Vacations are bare feet in warm sand.

If we hear a ringing telephone while on vacation, it's not for us. Need I say more?

The people we see, we won't see again. So if we decide to throw paper airplanes off the balcony of our fifth floor room, we don't have to worry about some irritable neighbor who, from that day on, will watch us carefully to see what we'll do next. We are freed from the expectations of others.

The family has the advantage of having both Mom *and* Dad present round the clock, day and night. What a concept! This alone seems to make for smoother family operations.

But our vacations are not always smooth. We've had vacations where someone was injured, or the car broke down in a remote location and we had to stay somewhere where there was nothing but a couple of broken-down rooms with bad plumbing. So it can't be that it's a carefree time.

So here's what it is, I've concluded, that makes vacations paradise on earth for me: It's that we all are together. At night I can hear everyone breathing (or snoring) nearby, whether we are in tents or in a room. There are no schedules or telephones to take us away from each other. For a short time each year we experience life as a cohesive unit. It doesn't seem to matter whether we experience Yosemite or Las Vegas (personally, I vote for Yosemite). It is our yearly growth period as we bond and learn to trust each other. The rest of the year, unfortunately, there is very little time to experience being a family. We're too busy working in order to be able to take a vacation.

A vacation is, in many ways, a kind of microcosm. It is a family striking out into the wilderness, finding roles to play to make the family work in new and sometimes unexpected situations. A play is also a kind of microcosm. It is a location, a time period, and a people, all existing, taking their roles to make it all work.

Two of my children had roles in a stake play, a massively professional presentation of *The Wizard of Oz.* Another son joined the stage crew, and I photographed. In the hours of rehearsing and creating I came to realize that something very real was created out of unorganized matter . . .

## *The Play's the Thing*

Audiences arrived on several different nights to see the magic. They came to see the play, and they were not disappointed. They sat in the dark and watched each act, each set change, and each actor. They were surprised, they were moved, and they laughed. At the end of each performance the smiling audience went home, satisfied that they had seen a complete play with a happy ending. What they didn't see was the real play.

The whole, complete, and real magic began several months earlier. One or two decided the play would be *The Wizard of Oz,* and then many gathered to accept roles, costume ideas, sheets of music, scripts, and visualizations. In time, more gathered. They came in all ages and sizes. They came from schools, homes, jobs, and from far away and nearby. They were experienced and inexperienced and every-thing in-between. The call to the stage carries no predeter-mined list. But one knows when one is called.

Lives were interrupted, the call was answered one by one, and then, six by six, they came, artists all, of one sort or another. And once fully gathered, in a short slice of time they created a universe.

Amid chaos, unorganized matter, and even at times a vir-tual vacuum, order and substance began to appear. It re-quired that each be committed to doing more than an indi-vidual's share. The product's total was to be far more than the sum of the parts. A synergy formed. Two plus two became sixteen as the angels rewarded effort.

In January there was an empty, dusty stage. In April there was Kansas and the empire of Oz. In January the occu-pants of the stage consisted only of a sleepy seminary stu-dent some weekday morning and a wandering toddler on a Sunday. In April the stage overflowed with the colorful citi-zens of entire civilizations.

In January there were some people talking about Oz. In April there was Dorothy and Toto, Uncle Henry and Aunt Em, witches and munchkins, winkies, poppies, monkeys, and no doubt in anyone's mind that a man had actually been made of tin.

After more hours than anyone had to spare spent sawing, painting, wiring, stitching, thinking, and rehearsing, a uni-verse was created in an adjacent dimension. And once it was far enough along in the stages of creation, the doors were opened and audiences were allowed to view the process of performing.

The remaining stages were not witnessed by the audi-ence: the striking of the set, the gathering of costumes, the removal of makeup, the reordering of matter. Nor was the audience aware of the final stages of creation that artists ex-perience, such as tears and the hollow empty spot in the heart that was previously occupied by an entire universe.

The audience simply came to see a play. They will say, "It wasn't real; it's only a play." But they'd be wrong. For a slice of time, Oz existed. The lion was real. Dorothy learned from her experiences. It was as real as real can ever be.

Dorothy always makes it back to Kansas eventually. But will middle-agers make it through child-rearing?

## The Purposes of Adolescence

I've often pondered the purposes of adolescence. The first time I pondered this was when I discovered myself to be an unwilling direct participant. Oh, I was willing when I was, say, eight or nine. I couldn't wait to be a teenager then. I thought there could be no station in life more glamorous than that. Then it arrived, and I found that there were a couple of details I hadn't expected.

Now that I'm a mom looking forward to the empty nest, I am pondering adolescence again. One of our children has made it through adolescence and we've all lived to tell about it, a fact that is nothing short of a miracle.

Another son has just about two years of adolescence left. So far so good, one might say. But even as I write this he is in the bathroom with about a half dozen of his friends dyeing his hair blue. My daughter comes out to see me from time to time, and the expression on her face is such that I am dreading seeing this son. He has been telling me for weeks that this is just a temporary thing that will be gone in a matter of days. Nevertheless, I have been saying that I do not condone this behavior in any way, shape, or form. (Although I am secretly relieved. Blue hair is not as bad as some other things that an adolescent might want to experience.) My husband remains neutral and reminds me of my own policy regarding the raising of adolescents. Allow them some safe rebellions here and there. It may prevent some major ones somewhere else.

And that is exactly why I must protest blue hair. It wouldn't be a rebellious act if he didn't have a parent saying, "Don't do that!"

My daughter has just come out to tell me that his hair is presently bright yellow because first he had to bleach it. I say, "Michael said this was a temporary thing. Doesn't he

know that bleach is permanent?" I hear all kinds of moans
and exclamations echoing from the bathroom. Another friend
enters through the front door, skateboard under his arm.
Once in the bathroom I hear him say, "That's so gross!
How're you going to get that out of your hair?" Words of comfort and cheer to Mom.

I turn to my keyboard. It's another one of those moments
when writing is more likely to keep me sane (and from com-
mitting some kind of rebellious act) than an activity like
folding towels, which I need to do . . . but I'm going to have to
get over this particular moment before I can once again feel
like an orderly domestic engineer. It takes a certain kind of
serene mind-set.

Another son will be turning thirteen in a few weeks.
We're already holding on tight, our knuckles white. He's
been taking us on a wild ride for at least a year already. Just
think, only seven more years to go.

I once spoke to a wise counselor in our stake presidency
about the subject of raising adolescents. I was interested in
hearing what words of wisdom he could offer me since he had
something like six kids, all of them adolescents to young
adults. And what's more, the eldest of the group seemed to be
turning out very nicely.

He took a deep breath and said, "I've learned that the
thing to concentrate on when they're all at that age is simply
damage control."

That's it? But as time has gone on I've seen the wisdom of
his words. The time to teach specific values and principles
tends to be over. After that it's like steering a runaway train;
the idea is to attempt to keep it going in the right direction
as much as possible and to prevent derailment.

And as far as the purpose of adolescence goes, I have considered that it is a time to try out identities, ponder, learn,
take on new responsibilities, and try on adult behaviors
while still safe within the confines of home. All that may be
true. But right now I am thinking of one other important
purpose of adolescence. I am remembering when my eldest
son shaved off one side of his head, left one side long, and
dyed that black. I am remembering when my third son took
firecrackers to school and sold them, and soon all kinds of

kids were letting them off and I had to go pick my son up from school and stay home with him a few days. And I am also thinking of my second son, who is still in the bathroom turning his ash blonde hair an unearthly shade of blue.

The purpose of adolescence might be to prompt parents to give that necessary nudge out of the nest. Imagine if there were no adolescence. Imagine our kids staying like sweet, co-operative nine-year-olds until age nineteen. Imagine them always looking up to us as if we knew something about life and they might want to listen. Wouldn't it be more difficult to send them off?

Adolescence is a time to allow parents to cut those apron strings. And then when our kids are, say, thirty-five, and no longer need to put all their energies into rebellious acts, we can invite them over for a visit. It will be so pleasant then that we will think of it as a reward for making it to that point, especially when they start telling us what *their* kids are doing.


When my kids are lamenting to me about the bizarre be-haviors of their children, I will be capable of exuding much compassion. Whether I will choose to exude it or not will de-pend, I think, upon whether I have gotten over all the things they did while I was on duty as their parent. Even if I do get over it, as much as that is possible, I may exude a tactful kind of compassion where I say, "Really? Your son stuck a screwdriver in the outlets and the entire house went dark and the outlet exploded, leaving a blackened wall? You must have been crazed [as I was when you did the same thing]." I suppose that is a kind of conditional compassion. There is, however, evidence that there is a kind of thing that could be called unconditional compassion . . .

## Compassion

I think the quality of pure, spontaneous compassion is overlooked. I hear some say that it doesn't exist, that people only do things to gain something for themselves. Or

I sometimes hear that one cannot have compassion until one has experienced much suffering in life.

My response is that I often see people doing things purely out of compassion, because they care, because they are fellow human beings in this experience called life. And if it takes experience to develop compassion, and indeed it may, then how does one explain the compassion of children?

My youngest two children were born in an alternative birth center. There were no drugs to make Mom or baby groggy. Only Dad was groggy. Immediately after birth they were turned over to their parents, and we all stayed together until we went home about twelve hours later.

During that twelve hours we slept and nursed and listened to Dad make countless phone calls. And there was something else that happened while we were there. Other babies were born. In a birth center room next door we heard the first cries of a newborn. In a delivery room down the hall we heard similar sounds. In each case we'd be touched at the sounds of the new life and we'd look at our own sleeping newborn. It happened every time. Our baby would also hear the cries and, in response, would pucker up and give a few little cries too.

One can argue that they cried because their sleep was interrupted, or that they were irritated at the sound, or that it reminded them of what they'd just come through and they were afraid it wasn't over yet. But ask any mother. The infant's cries certainly seem to be cries of empathy.

When my number two son was only a few months away from his due date, my number one son was approaching his second birthday. The two of us were living alone in a cold climate that winter. He came down with the stomach flu, and I stayed by his side for the two days it took for it to run its course. Finally he was well again, and we settled down for the first good night's rest in some time. But at three in the morning I awoke with the certain knowledge that I had it.

I was miserable, hanging over the toilet, when I felt a small hand patting my back. He had crawled out of his crib and come to comfort me. He did many of the things I had done for him. He wiped my brow, led me back to my bed, and went to get a bucket for me.

A friend told me that his wife sent him to pick up their daughter after work. She had been playing at a friend's house. He waited near the front door for what seemed to be hours. The child's mother apologized and said something about a lost doll and disappeared again. My friend was determined to be cheerful and patient, so he waited and resisted the urge to stomp off and physically remove his daughter to the car. His patience was rewarded later as they were on the way home.

"So, it took you so long because you were helping your friend find her doll?" he asked, the epitome of patience.

"Dad, the doll is *lost!*" His daughter was not as patient with her dense father. "I was helping her *cry!*"

When my brother and his family came to visit us they spent a night at our house and one in an Anaheim hotel near Disneyland. When they returned to their home in Pocatello I got a telephone call from them. It seems that their youngest child left his special blanket behind at the hotel. While the adults were doing their best to trace the blanket, with a detailed description of its flannel softness and the baby bears in diapers depicted on its surface, my daughter was busy feeling compassion for her cousin. The first few nights she asked me questions about how her little cousin was doing without his special blanket. On another night she decided to intentionally put her own special blanket in the wash. The next morning she revealed that she did it to see what it must be like for her cousin. Her conclusion was that it wasn't easy.

Her cousin was in another state and couldn't fully realize what compassion my daughter was experiencing; at least, not in a concrete fashion. Perhaps children readily feel compassion because they are in a state of dependence. They readily see the connections between all of us. Our compassionate feelings connect and support us in ways we can never fully know or see, but can feel. It wouldn't surprise me if my nephew felt a moment of calm in the midst of his loss, a moment when another carried his burden for a while.

# PART THREE

———❖———

# The Three Inevitables:
# Death, Taxes, and
# Parent-Teacher
# Conferences

*(The Self Versus the State)*

———————❖———————

Could there be anything more inevitable than middle age itself? While one may wish to skip such an awkward stage, one simply cannot earn one's rights as a senior citizen, with all its discounts, without paying one's dues.

And what might those dues be? Work, taxes, mortgages, braces, and love handles are among them. The responsibilities are heavy, and the light at the end of the tunnel is nowhere in sight. Pretty depressing, huh?

Not to worry. There are some perks. I'm sure there are. Well, okay, maybe they're not really obvious. I suppose you could say they just kind of sneak up on us when we're not looking. Maybe what is needed is an exploration of the self verses the state. The state of middle age, that is, with all its institutions.

Perhaps we could begin with the eternal state of adolescence as it is visited upon each of our children.

Eternity is an inevitability. A teen with headphones that will need to be surgically removed after what has seemed an eternal adolescence is also an inevitability . . .

## Circles

When my daughter was about to turn eight years old she very solemnly told me that for her birthday she would like "a Walkman and a Paula Abdul tape."

Taken by surprise at this request, and assuming that it was likely influenced by her association with classmates of various stages of development and worldliness, I sat down with her to discuss the matter.

I explained that there is so much music in the world and that childhood is so short. I explained that soon enough she'd be a teenager and that there was no good reason for hurrying to that stage.

I used my hands to demonstrate the length of her first ten years in comparison to her remaining seventy or eighty years. I explained that those first ten years would have a profound effect on those remaining years . . . which appeared as an eternity to her, so now was the time to make the most of it.

There is so much music to hear, and she might, I explained, get stuck with only one kind during her teenage years (years and years!), so now was the time to hear what kinds of choices there were. Now was the time for tapes of Mozart and Bach and even jazz and Judy Collins singing lullabies.

And as I held out my hands to demonstrate the shortness of the childhood years when compared to the remaining years to emphasize how those short years would affect those long years, I suddenly saw the metaphor I had created. I saw how our earth years are like our short formative years, and how much our earth experience will affect our eternal lives.

I looked at her and saw that she was also understanding, but at a level which was different from the level at which I was understanding it. And I realized that the distinction was not important. We are eternal sisters, growing and going in ever expanding circles.

We are brothers and we are sisters, even when we can't get ahold of each other. Many us of don't stay in one place for very long, except maybe while in the grocery store . . .

# Dear RS President:
# RE: Visiting Teaching

I realize that there is no other women's organization on the face of the earth that has been in existence longer than our good old RS. And I am pleased to belong to an organization that does so much good. And then there is the visiting teaching system. Yes, it is indeed wonderful that every woman in the organization has her own visiting friend or two to check on her, see how she's doing, bring her dinner when she's sick, share her sorrows when she mourns, and bring her chocolate chip cookies when she diets.

All of this is well and good. I have just one little concern. Why is it, as it seems to me, that the women I am assigned to visit have different schedules than mine? And why is it that the women assigned to visit me and offer me relief and empathy are playing telephone tag with me more than they are visiting me?

Perhaps we could improve this system by grouping women together in a more convenient fashion. For instance. My neighbor and I must speak to each other a minimum of thirty-two hours per week, just in the course of a typical week. I mean, my kids are over at her house and I'm calling her to ask her if it's true that she has offered each of them a root bear float and a movie (she did). And she is calling to see if I did indeed agree to take them all to Disneyland (I didn't).

If I were her visiting teacher, and if she were mine, we'd know if there were any special needs.

Or you could give Judy to me, or me to Judy. I thought this one through just the other day. I was in the supermarket, feeling guilty that I hadn't reached Carol, the woman I'm assigned to watch out for. I went down the first aisle, my nose buried in my list, and nearly bumped into Judy.

We greeted each other and made some kind of cheerful remark (we'd both just begun to shop, so we weren't discouraged yet). I saw her again on the paper goods aisle and we talked about some problems she was having.

When we met on the cereal aisle we discussed the fact that the cereal boxes were shrinking in size while the prices were creeping up. We concluded that if they didn't want anyone to notice the shrinking boxes, they might need to move the shelves close together.

By the time we met in the frozen foods section we were both feeling a little down. We talked about the challenges of feeding a family on a budget. By the time we'd completed our shopping we'd had a complete visit. "Hey," I said to Judy, "too bad you're not my visiting teacher. We could call this a visit!"

And so, dear RS president. If you want the cogs to turn more smoothly, may I suggest more convenient assignments?

What's that? You're saying it wasn't meant to be convenient? Oh, I see. Perhaps a little sacrifice makes service sweeter. More meaningful? Okay.

Well, would you mind if I were to ask Carol when and where she does her grocery shopping?


Perhaps if we can't find each other at the grocery store, we might find each other at the polling booths. Perhaps we could do our visiting teaching once every presidential election? I didn't think so. Well, there's always the tradition that my husband and I honor each election day . . .

## *What a Country!*

What a country! Only a democracy like this could provide us with so many opportunities, so many choices, and so much confusion. I am beginning to hope my ballot will have an additional choice this year: "None of the above."

As candidates square off and debate over personalities and pasts and evade important issues, I get more and more confused.

If that's not enough, I've heard that there are initiatives on the ballot that will cancel each other out if they aren't voted just right. One must read the voter's pamphlet carefully.

Mine just arrived today. *Pamphlet???* What a misnomer! Perhaps we should vote on what to call it:

_____A book
_____A directory
_____A catalog
_____A reference volume
_____A doorstop

It's time for me to devote several months to deciphering the—until we choose a better word—pamphlet. Confusion is, I suppose, a necessary but temporary side effect of freedom. I may be confused, but I am blessed to have choices. And I can alleviate my confusion by studying the issues and seeking divine guidance.

And once I've figured it out, I'll walk with my husband to my neighborhood polling place. We'll each enter a booth and exercise our rights as citizens of this land of the free.

On our walk home, we'll feel glad we've made our voices heard, until we discover, through further discussion, that we've canceled each other's votes.

What a country!


My husband and I are politically incompatible, but that doesn't mean we can't celebrate the rarely mentioned and little known phenomenon known as . . .

## *Middle-Age Love*

You'd think that love is something that can only be experienced by those who meet the prerequisites: young, attractive, and trendy. That's what commercials, billboards, movies, and advertisements scream at us over and over again.

But it's like the difference between a party animal doing his thing and a grandpa peering down at his first grandchild for the first time. Who is having more fun? The grandpa. But try to tell that to the party animal who is loudly proclaiming his fun and thinks that's as good as it gets. The noisier, flashier thing is what gets noticed.

How long can a love last if it's based upon how young, attractive, or trendy the love object is? Only for a noisy flash.

There is (surprise!) such a thing as over-the-hill, middle-age love, contrary to popular media opinion.

It is many hours of time logged side by side with a spouse. It can include taking each other for granted a few too many times, and the routine can be dull at times. Some long hours can be full of only sorrow, hard work, and/or trepidation, punctuated occasionally by flashes of joy.

But it is these many routine hours together that make it real when apart from each other. Then there is the missing of the other and the appreciating of the other. And then, when one of us spots the other across some distance and through a crowd, there is an attraction that draws us back. A magnetic power built upon shared experiences, both the joyful and the sorrowful.

In time, joy grows like a cushion that supports and envelops; it is steady, quiet, and sure.

There is no youth nor perfume that can create a stronger bond than that.

If there is an attraction that is little understood between long-term couples, then there must also surely be some kind of instinctive homing tendency within us . . .

## HOME CALLING

Concrete, signs—"DO NOT ENTER," "NO RIGHT TURN"—
Hard edges, hard glances, impatient crowds,
Red lights, broken glass, untrusting eyes,
Shoppers rushing to embellish their exteriors,
Clanging voices, aggressive drivers, shortchanging,
Short-tempered, smokey hacks, grease and gum.

So far from home, driving and praying,
Every intersection passed a blessing.
Turn right, turn left, flashing orange,
Road construction, bus fumes, squealing tires,
Rubber fumes, robber blues.

Home calling, implanted navigational instinct,
Invisible thread pulling, I face home
Like a compass facing north, no matter what,
Through concrete and asphalt, stay stressed,
Stay tuned, stay alert, follow the rules.

Slipping into home at last, it smiles
And welcomes inward to sigh
And sink into safety, this refuge
Where the edges are softened and
My nerves reattach to solid
Stability and I wonder why I
Ever left in the first place.

Our homes and the families that inhabit them may not be perfect, but it is when we are there that we can be the most comfortable. It is the fold where we can express fears and celebrate triumphs. Our ward can also be like a family, once we come to accept each other . . .

## *The New Bishop and the Loose Tooth*

It was a fairly quiet sacrament meeting. Maybe it was because most of the deacons were away at a Scout camp. Or it might have been because we had a new bishop. Perhaps some were more quiet than usual because of the novelty of new faces conducting. It's also possible that it was quiet because some were observing the new bishop. Some may have been sizing him up, wondering how he would be as father of the ward.

Our family sat behind the new bishop's family. Or at least we sat behind the bishop's wife and the three daughters. The son sat at the sacrament table, and, of course, the bishop sat at the pulpit so we could all get a good look at him in his new calling.

As the new counselor made some announcements he included his announcement that he was nervous. A sigh of empathy rippled down the rows. It was new to us too. There seemed to be a slight tension in the air. It was as if the new bishopric was doing its best to make a seamless transition from the last great bishopric by being as polished as possible.

Then life stepped in to subtly interrupt. We saw the bishop's young daughter showing her mom her very loose tooth. Her mom smiled and smoothed the girl's hair. We saw her father watching her from his lofty position and smile too. Then we saw her parents turn their attention elsewhere. But the little girl's attention was still focused on that loose tooth, and she was determined to have it out and done with.

We saw her tugging and twisting at it for quite some time while the counselor stood at the microphone apologizing sincerely for massacring someone's name. She continued to work at the tooth, unobserved except by us. We had the best view of the drama that was unfolding. Suddenly the tooth was freed. It happened very quietly, but it was as if every member of her family was connected to her with some kind of eternal language that didn't need words. Her mom turned in time to see the daughter proudly holding aloft the tooth. Her mom's smile included an element of surprise, and she looked up to see the son at the sacrament table also smiling.

In turn, the bishop beamed from his vantage point. If the power of love could be seen, the ward members would've seen bright laser beams shooting across the chapel from one family member to the other. All of this took place in silence, but it nevertheless shuddered through the family like a buoyant hymn.

Some might say that that wasn't very reverent. Perhaps the family needed to postpone that loose tooth for a more appropriate time (as if life can be postponed). But it is my own personal feeling that the Lord will, of course, forgive and also rejoice with this family because they were following a higher law. They were loving one another.

Any bishop who will notice something as tiny as his young daughter's tooth coming out when he is sitting up there above the congregation is a bishop, I feel, who is on the right track. He has my heartfelt sustaining vote.

———❖———

We are fortunate that we have the opportunity to extend our families to those around us, if we choose to do so. My ward family became an incredible support to me when my father passed away suddenly. Coming home, I found a cushion of messages and offers of support. Without that support, I wonder how I would have managed. Because ward members filled in for me by performing many of my daily duties and obligations, I was able to slow down, spend some time in contemplation, and say good-bye . . .

## Good-Bye, Dad

It was kind of a sad project to remove the ornaments from the tree the morning of New Year's Eve. But then my mom called and told me that my dad died that morning.

The bare tree abandoned, I packed to go to my mother, and mourned my father's sudden passing. I imagined the scene she described of finding him. It seemed that he rose up in his dying and shed his well-used and weary physical body, as if he'd stepped out of it and left it where his spirit shed it.

There was no lingering illness taking him away bit by bit. He was full of life and excitement about learning new things. Christmas had brought many visitors, including grandchildren who bathed him in their unconditional adoration, and he spent many hours playing with exciting new computer programs.

All was well, and then he went, leaving behind all the evidence of a full and active life. And we bumped into each other's tears and struggled to fill the gaping hole he left in our lives with chatter, memories, sobs, and laughter.

We began to understand, if reluctantly, that what he taught us by his living is that life is indeed a challenge and, at times, terrible, but nevertheless, a wondrous thing.

"The world is full of a number of things, I think we should all be as happy as kings!" is the kind of phrase (this one borrowed from Robert Louis Stevenson) I often heard him say. That and, "Here, eat these raw onions, they're good for you!"

And so, the Christmas ornaments are all sealed up in boxes, and who knows where they disappeared to out in the garage. It seems like it will be a long time before I see them again . . . but Christmas will arrive again faster than I expect.

And dear Father, you are going away where I won't see you for a while. For those ornaments, the sadness is just a fleeting moment. For you, it is tremendous. And I must rely upon my faith that I will see you again.

Until then I'll remember that "the world is full of a number of things," raw onions being one that I'll pass on.

Until then I'll remember that what matters most is each other.

Until then I'll look at life with eternal perspective.

Until then, good-bye.

Our eternal relationships are something we can enjoy (and be mystified, exasperated, and annoyed about) in this life and the next. But our material possessions are not. So why, then, are we taking precious time away from our families to go shopping? (Okay, other than to get a break when they are mystifying, exasperating, and annoying us.)

### THE BUY DANCE

Hurry, scurry, buy.
Hook it on your arm.
It's the latest, greatest,
Hurry and buy
While it's still the latest, greatest.

Soon it will be replaced,
Here come the new styles,
Jump up
Hurry, scurry, buy
Wrap it around you.
It's the neatest, completest,

Oops!
It's out of style.
Don't be caught dead with it,
Give it away quickly.
Get the newest,
Hurry, scurry, buy. . . .

I think, if you don't mind,
I'll sit out a dance or two.

Perhaps we seek to embellish ourselves as a quick route to self-improvement. A new shirt, a bright color, anything new or different. Perhaps a professional makeover. Anything better than what we've got or who we are. But maybe we have been taking too much for granted. Maybe, if given the chance, we can find things to like just the way they are . . .

## *Makeover*

My husband and I were chosen for a couples makeover that was to be aired on a morning television program. Six couples were chosen late one weeknight after hundreds of us were asked to appear at the studio. We drove home from the Hollywood lot exhausted, excited, and in a kind of stupor at what we had ahead of us. We would get home late that night, and we'd have to be at the studio by seven the next morning to prepare for that morning's broadcast. We had to arrange for childcare and everything else between the time we got home and the time we'd have to leave in the morning.

And if that wasn't enough to boggle the mind, we were asked to arrive at the studio wearing something blah. We were also asked to not do anything with our hair, and the women were asked to come without makeup (the men, too, for that matter). They wanted us to appear on the air as blah-types. All the way home I kept repeating, "I'm going to appear on live television with no makeup on a program watched by millions?" It was as if I needed to question my sanity. Little did I know how much my sanity-questioning foreshadowed what was to come.

Sure enough, we all appeared in front of the cameras looking as blah as we normally would at that hour without a little help from the cosmetic industry. They took some "before" pictures. "Don't smile," the photographer told me. I tried to look like a poor, haggard soul desperately in need of a makeover, while the studio execs looked on to be sure I did. It really wasn't that hard after four hours of sleep and no shampoo.

Of course, there were guests sharing the green room with

us. The one I remember the most was Ted Danson, only because the other women were in agony over his presence: "My one chance to meet Ted Danson, and I look like I crawled out from under a rock!" At the end of the show we were herded out to wave good-bye to the cameras, and once the cameras were off it was down to business.

The makeover artist took my husband and me to a West Hollywood mall where, each in turn, she threw clothes at us. I found myself in a dressing room, and she brought me things I would never wear, like bright red sweaters with polka dots the size of Frisbees and shoulder pads as big as toy poodles. Finally she chose for me a bright purple blazer with a fuchsia skirt made of a synthetic fabric that would wither and dissolve if someone accidentally spilt water on it. Then she rushed me over to a posh department store to get shoes. She picked out leather pumps in fuchsia that cost what we spend to feed a family of six for seven days.

The shopping frenzy completed, we were instructed to meet immediately at a Beverly Hills hair salon. We found it in a hilly area with lots of trees and curving streets. The interior was full of bushy plants and terra-cotta tile. There was a star hairdresser and his underlings. It was easy to tell who the star-hair-guy was; he was the one who was charging four hundred dollars for a trim, and the newly trimmed gave him kisses in spite of it. I was glad to know I would not be giving him either.

I was plunked into a seat to be examined. The star-hair-guy was lifting my hair and examining it. The colorist was looking at it as if it had just been injured in a hit-and-run. The makeover artist was telling them that she felt that because I spent too much time out of doors I had become "over-blonded." She imagined something more "earthy." All three of them considered my head as if they might find the solution to all the world's problems therein.

Getting bored, I looked around. I saw a very ugly woman with foil all over her head. She was about six feet tall, with a craggy nose and jutting jaw. Her hands were huge and gangly. She was reading movie mags.

I was soon changed into a black robe; offered tea, cappuccino, or wine (I settled for water); and told that lunch would be served pretty soon. Lunch served? I wondered if they ran the place like an airline. Would this be a lunch haircut? Maybe next time I'd book a dinner haircut. The next thing I knew I was being shampooed, at last, and then my head was massaged for a good ten minutes. I hadn't expected that. I kept trying to get up, but the massage wasn't over yet.

The star-hair-guy and his assistants then cut my hair for a solid hour and a half. I had no idea anyone could spend that much time on one haircut. They must have cut each hair individually. I kept thinking, *Any minute now they'll be finished,* but no-o-o-o.

Finally I was moved to another station. When I got there I saw that my haircut was not bad, kind of a chin-length bob with very subtle layers giving my normally stick-straight, boring hair some texture. I also saw my husband in another chair, his head covered in foil. And I saw lots of empty pizza boxes. I had missed lunch! When I asked if anything was left, they brought me a pickle. My hunger whetted, I leaned toward my husband, "Pssst . . . let's get out of here!" He just threw a foil ball at me.

I was serious. I get antsy if my haircut goes on for more than five minutes. I always feel like I am trapped and out of control when I am in a hair establishment. There's no telling what they could do to you in a place like that. My instincts, I later discovered, were on the mark.

The colorist spent what seemed like three days wrapping my hair in foil. I saw countless bobbed heads coming and going, flashing hundred dollar bills and giving kisses. I saw the ugly woman getting her freshly highlighted hair dried and brushed. Her long, layered hair flowed and glowed. Then she got up and I realized she . . . he was a heavy metal rock star. I hoped to look as good when I walked out.

I sat with my head wrapped in foil and cotton under a hair dryer, feeling like I'd rather be giving birth. My ears were hot, I couldn't move, and there wasn't anything within reach that was worth reading. It was getting dark. How long had I been under the dryer? Did they ever forget someone under the dryer and go home?

Finally I was ushered back to the shampoo area. I was relieved to think my ordeal would soon be over. I was shampooed and massaged again, and brought back to my chair. Someone began to dry my hair, and to my horror I saw that I had been transformed into a carrot top. I could've auditioned for the lead in *Annie.*

"Uh," I gulped, "Isn't it a little . . . uh . . . *bright?*"

"It's hard to tell before we get it dry," the colorist said, but she definitely looked worried.

I felt my spirits sinking. *I'm about to appear before millions of viewers with Day-Glo orange hair,* I thought. I looked around for my husband, but he was nowhere in sight.

My hair was dry, and if anything it was an even brighter shade of orange. The colorist began to rub chemicals into my hair, the kind designed to remove hair color. The odor was threatening enough to eradicate the nerve endings required for a sense of smell. I was back at the shampoo bowl. The shampoo girl seemed to be losing patience; she scrubbed and then she cut the massage part down to eight minutes.

I was back in the colorist's chair. She seemed to feel as disturbed as I felt. This time my hair was a lighter but just as intense Day-Glo orange. "Could it be just toned down?" I asked tentatively, afraid to have anything else done, but also afraid to have Day-Glo hair.

Dark brown goo was applied to my hair in huge amounts. It dripped down my neck. I was back under the dryer, wishing I had skipped out when my instincts told me to.

Back to the shampoo lady, who could barely disguise her weariness. My neck was getting sore from leaning back in the shampoo bowl, my scalp was getting sore, and she cut her massage down to a mere five minutes.

With my hair dried, I looked up and was startled to see a person with hair so muddy dark that her fair skin looked deathly pale. I looked like I'd slipped into an oil slick. "Pretty dark, huh?" I said, trying to remain cheerful. I looked like I needed CPR. On top of the oily darkness was a deep burgundy sheen.

My husband returned. He'd gone to dinner without me. I don't know which made me more upset, that he'd gone for actual food and didn't bring me any, or that he had gone out to breathe the free air while I remained the imprisoned torture victim of the colorist.

"Hey," he said with the cheerfulness of one who has breathed freely and eaten a meal, "I've always liked redheads!"

He meant to cheer me up. It didn't work. All I could think of was that not only had someone made me look like an Irish Setter that drowned in an oil slick, now my husband reveals that he likes redheads, something I am not, whether a colorist attempts to make me one or not. I couldn't take any more. Tears began to slide down my face. My nose turned as red as my hair, only a more becoming shade.

The colorist agreed that it was pretty "heavy." Out came the foil, and it seemed that a month later (and one more trip to the head-immobilizing-heat-contraption, where I looked at a magazine featuring the heavy metal star leaping on a stage, sans foil headdress—no wonder they call it heavy metal) I was heading back for the dreaded shampoo bowl. I noticed that the back of my head was very tender from my frequent trips to the bowl, and the shampoo girl's massage was reduced to a paltry three minutes and her heart wasn't in it.

Back to the colorist, I found my hair was a heavy burgundy (as in funeral-dark velvet) laced with orange streaks. I was miserable. The colorist said that was the best she could do. I resisted suggesting that she could've just left me alone. They closed up shop. I changed out of my black robes, crying angry tears, and went home. At home I left a message for the makeover expert, who was still out on the town enjoying looking like a normal human being. I told her that there was no way that I would be willing to appear in front of the cameras looking like Morticia Addams after dipping her black hair in Easter egg orange dye.

When she called back the next morning she was full of good cheer, telling me that if I would go back to the hair salon they would gladly return me to a normal hair color. I grabbed some photographs of myself with my real hair color to guide them.

When I walked into the salon, the makeover expert exclaimed incredulously, "You don't like it?"

I thought she must be putting me on. "Uh . . . no." She asked why, and I listed a few things, such as the color—

which was nothing like anything that grows out of any scalp on earth—and the fact that it made me look like Elvira's puny sister.

"Oh, but all you have to do is use different makeup. I'll show you; with orange-tone makeup you'll look fabulous."

Great. First they change my hair to a foreign tone, now they'll change my skin to match. What next? Colored contact lenses so my eyes will match my new hair color and skin color? I could see where this could lead. "Actually . . ." I countered, "I thought maybe something closer to my natural color." I brought forth the photographs.

The makeover expert, the colorist, and the star-hair-guy all examined the photographs with expressions that one might have if looking at photographs of rare skin disorders. "You can't have that!" the makeover expert exclaimed. "Your natural color is too dull for television!"

After recovering from that, it struck me. So that's what it's all about? It's "for television." It's all for show. These makeovers are not for improving the lives of the made-over. They're for flash and entertainment.

The following Monday my husband and I made our way to Hollywood so we could be displayed as new and improved. I watched out the window and saw graffiti, gangs, and homeless people waking up on their bus benches, throwing off their newspaper quilts. *Here are people living a harsh drama,* I thought, *and I am about to appear on live television wearing a pair of fuchsia pumps with a price tag that would be the equivalent of many meals to these people. The stores gave the shoes and the clothes away just for the show, for the flash, the entertainment, and a mention of their product on the air.*

At the studio I was dressed in my showy outfit, makeup was applied, and the star-hair-guy and two assistants spent an hour blow-drying and styling my hair. I saw it all through skeptical eyes.

In front of the cameras the makeover expert talked so much I couldn't get a word in edgewise. I think she was afraid I'd blow her cover. They put my scowling "before" on the screen next to my astonishing "after," and the audience oohed and ahhed. The makeover expert explained that I had been "over-blonded" and they wanted to give me a more "sophisticated look."

Next they brought out my husband. He was stunning in a suit, and they had highlighted his hair with blonde. "He's a Californian," the makeover expert explained, "so we wanted to give him that healthy beach look." I'm sure the camera cut away from my face. I get the Morticia look and he gets the healthy beach look? What is wrong with this picture?

Then it got even more interesting. She brought out some instrument of torture that I'd never seen before. "This was used on Casey's hair to give it that smooth look." It was? "Sometimes it's hard to get that smooth look, so this straightens the hair." My hair is already about as straight as hair can possibly be; it grows that way all by itself.

"So you can highlight his hair," the show's host suggested to me, "and he can straighten yours."

The makeover expert jumped in before I could say anything. "And we'll give her one to take home with her." She waved the hair straightening device (no pun intended) in front of my face.

During the week that followed our makeover adventure I managed to take back my acetate dry-clean-only-or-it-will-melt outfit. I exchanged it for some real clothes in cotton. I took back the fuchsia pumps and exchanged them for a pair of Reeboks. The leftover credit was blown on food and bills. I did lose some hair. It kind of melted like the outfit would have. But fortunately it grew back defiantly.

So I learned my lesson about superficial appearances and all-for-show phoniness. My hair is my normal, not-for-television color again. I still have and wear the clothes I got by exchanging the fake clothes. The only thing I don't have is that strange appliance for straightening hair. I never saw it after it was brandished like a weapon for the television cameras. It was not given to me as I was promised on the air.

That's okay, I have no need for it in real life. It was just "for television," a place where my hair color is too dull. I never realized how peaceful dull can be.

Television might dazzle, but all the flash is in the front, the part everyone sees. Television producers don't have time for more than the facade. They're probably too busy with other things . . .

I'm not certain how our time will be spent in the future, but I am aware that we are presently living in the era of the timesaving device. Then why is it that we have even less time than our ancestors?

## *Timesaving (Or "Unplugged")*

Welcome to the era of the timesaving device. Never before in history has humankind been so free to pursue the ever evasive dream. And it's all due to our modern technology. Yes, computers, microwaves, answering machines, and all manner of miraculous inventions have liberated us from the enslavement of tedium. Then how come we're more pressed for time than ever before?

Let us explore a few of the most familiar time-savers:

*Computers.* They are wonderful. One can type one letter and with just a few strokes of the keyboard or a few mouse clicks one can change the name of the addressee, and voila, one can be caught up on a year's worth of correspondence. Then there are address labels, shopping lists, budget records, spreadsheets, graphics. Why, one's little ones can be plunked in front of the computer to learn touch typing, algebra, reading, and chess, freeing one to pursue other things, like reading the microwave manual.

But along with the computer's timesaving features there are some hefty time-consuming activities that one must submit to in order to fully take advantage of all the computer's timesaving features. To put it simply, everything one can imagine about the computer, from memory to hard drive to mouse to software, and every single program, comes with its own set of literature. The literature ranges from a manual about the size of a best-selling paperback (and one-sixteenth as readable) to a set as large as all thirty volumes of the *Encyclopedia Britannica* (and just as detailed). If the average computer user with just the average amount of software were to lay the manuals acquired with the computer and software along the ground, one after another, the manuals would extend the diameter of the earth three times. Not even the timesaving features of the computer will free up enough time for the computer user to read that much. And so, a microwave becomes a necessity.

*Microwaves.* These babies cook so fast that they make one impatient waiting for toast to brown in the toaster. They are great for heating milk for hot chocolate and for reheating leftovers. They also do a wonderful job of cooking little trays of frozen entrees that never look anything at all like the picture on the outside of the package.

It's a good thing microwaves do such a good job of cooking supermarket fast food in a hurry, because one must work overtime to pay for the thing. And while one slaves away to pay for the "nuke-it" device, the answering machine will take messages.

*Answering machines.* A miraculous invention. Not only do they allow one to go take a walk, knowing that calls will be recorded, they also allow one to ignore the phone while eating dinner. And even more than that, when there is a message from the Primary president on Friday, one can assume that she is desperate for someone to teach the six- and seven-year-olds since the last four teachers won't return her calls, and one can have time to find something else to do next Sunday before calling her back. Now that's a time-saver *and* a sanity saver.

But one might think twice when one comes home after a stressful day and notes that there are thirty-four messages on the machine. Then one must take time to listen to them all, writing notes on who called whom and all the who's, what's, where's, when's, and return phone numbers. And then one must squeeze into the next few days (as more calls continue to be recorded) a long list of people who are expecting a return call. If one had no answering machine, one would return home blissfully ignorant that anyone had called at all.

And then there's "telephone tag." One can get a good game of that going that can last for weeks, and there are those names and numbers on the list that are carried over from week to week until the game of tag finally ends. One might be tempted, in this case, to drive to the home of the fellow tag player and wait until they come home. Good thing there is a car.

*Cars.* Yes, they save time. Imagine having to walk ten miles to a supermarket, carrying the provisions home in a backpack. It would take up most of the day. With a motorized vehicle one can make it to the part-time job, the supermarket, the PTA meeting, the vet, the pediatrician, and the Relief Society board meeting (after dropping one child off to Scouts and another to Mutual) all in one day!

But who wants to do that? If one had no vehicle one could stay home more ("I can't do that; you see, I have no car!") and knit a sweater instead. Or read the VCR manual.

*VCRs.* It's exciting to think that when one is too busy to watch a few good programs during the week, one can, with just a few buttons, record all those programs to be watched at another time.

But the excitement begins to fade as one sees the recorded programs stack up unwatched because there is still no time. Soon one notices there are tapes with dates written on them indicating they were taped eight years ago. And soon one begins to fantasize having a broken leg to allow some down time. After deeper consideration, however, one decides instead to simply stack all those unwatched tapes on top of all those unread computer manuals.

Our exploration of timesaving technology is far from complete, but it will suffice. Only a few examples are needed to demonstrate why, with all our timesaving devices, we have less time.

It's not just that the timesaving devices require time in some form or another, however. It seems to me that one of the biggest problems is that so much more is expected of us. Our ancestors may have been more realistic about what could be accomplished in one day. They were limited by time, travel, and terrain. They had no telephones and no photocopied schedules handed to them. Physical limitations kept them at a more sane pace. And they still had time at the end of the day, if they weren't too tired, to play a fiddle and tell some stories.

We, however, living in an age of miracles, expect miracles. A package can arrive overnight, passengers can be in Paris by daybreak, we can speak on the telephone to someone in Hong Kong, the freeway can take us across several counties (and in some parts of the country, several states) in an hour or two, we can look up a library book with a modem, order a gift by telephone, bake a potato in five minutes. Why, then, shouldn't we be able to pull together a Primary sacrament meeting with thirty-two speaking parts and five new songs in fifteen days?

I have no solutions, other than maybe we could all try to wedge a few spaces between all our busy-ness, take some time off occasionally (without having to break a leg), and . . . maybe we could unplug everything now and then.


Sometimes we don't have to unplug anything. Sometimes appliances simply quit on their own, usually the day the warranty expires. Or after a decade or two of marriage. The other night I sat through a lengthy baby shower which revealed, after all the brightly wrapped packages were opened, enough baby clothes to open an outlet, "Baby Boyz R Us." Someone approaching her twentieth wedding anniversary said, "Hey, why don't *we* get showers anymore? I could really use some towels!" I smiled, thinking about the bathroom rug that would probably disintegrate in the next wash and the terrible groaning sounds our refrigerator has been making in its last, gasping days. Our items of living have taken a beating. Maybe we need to rethink our shower etiquette . . .

## *Wedding Gifts*

The toaster has gone berserk. Even though there are dials that indicate the type of item being toasted (generally bread-type items, no listing for marshmallows) and the exact degree of toasting one might wish for, in the end there are really only two choices: toasted on one side and black on the other, or slightly warm bread.

The telephone has joined the mutiny. It switches to a dial tone whenever it pleases, which is often in the middle of a conversation with a school principal. The telephone's mood swings force us to apologize to callers the moment we get on the phone. "The telephone is acting up; it may cut us off at any moment," we say (and consider telling that to telephone solicitors even after the telephone is fixed).

Several plastic food containers have lost their lids either to the great black hole (where favorite socks are also snatched mercilessly from their mates) or to the dishwasher melt-down cycle. Where are wedding gifts when we need them?

Oh sure, we once had cute little food containers with matching lids, three toasters, and an actual full set of matching glasses. There were cloth napkins, dish towels, and salt and pepper shakers. I bet we even had eight spoons.

We had the accouterments of marriage and family life when we didn't really need them, except to examine the dinner plates and imagine ourselves enjoying them at a table full of quiet, appreciative offspring. (Weren't we naive?)

But where are those niceties now? Now is when we've got kids coming and going in shifts, meals needing to be stored neatly for a latecomer, and enough telephone traffic to warrant a switchboard. Now is when we're toasting waffles, muffins, and even toast on the run. Now is when we need all the help we can get. These days we're grabbing jelly jars featuring Garfield and Fred Flintstone and sliding them across a bare table set with paper towels working overtime as napkins.

It seems to me that a solution would be for us to simply begin a new, more sensible tradition. This could be accomplished in several creative ways. One would be for the newly-to-be-wed couple to state on their invitations: "Gifts will be postponed until our fifteenth anniversary."

Then, when they are dealing with appliances, children, and meals and spills night and day, they will truly appreciate that new toaster or set of food containers . . . with lids.

Another solution would be for wedding guests to give gift certificates such as: "This gift certificate is good for one set of brightly colored dish towels, when you really need them." Or:

"When you are forty-ish and dealing with teenagers who never do what you wish them to do, this gift certificate is good for one new toaster that will do exactly what you want!"

We may as well have toasters that do what we want, because we sure don't have eyes that do what we want anymore . . .

## *Milestone*

As a child growing up there were many milestones that I looked forward to. There was the first slumber party, first pair of high heels (a whopping one-inch heel, but I wobbled nonetheless), first dance, and first date.

There was that first, very strange, day of college (BYU dorms seemed like dungeons at first, and then there was registration at the Smith Field House—I can still smell the sawdust), and much later, that first pregnancy, which had me turning my nose up at all kinds of formerly beloved foods.

All of these kinds of milestones were worthy of noting and were accompanied by various degrees of fanfare.

Now that I've passed the big 4-0 I notice that not only have the milestones changed considerably, but I am left on my own to note them, reluctantly.

While the milestone of getting my first pair of heels was something that had me champing at the bit and had my mother pulling back on the reins, the opposite seems to be happening with middle-age milestones. And those first heels brought my friends around to giggle and to show me their heels, and we attempted to walk as if we'd always worn them, showing off while attempting to be nonchalant. We seem to prefer to keep a low profile with these new milestones.

For several years my optometrist has been telling me that I need to consider getting reading glasses. And I've been saying, "Why? I'm nearsighted. I can read just fine." He would just look amused. I couldn't figure it out. If I'm nearsighted, why would I need reading glasses?

But each time I saw the optometrist he seemed increasingly amused and he'd make references about "eyes over forty." But I didn't want to listen. It wouldn't be fair to be nearsighted most of your life and then become farsighted too!

Soon I was questioning the optometrist, "What do you mean? Wear reading glasses *over* my contact lenses?" And I was walking out thinking, *These guys just want to find any opportunity they can to sell more glasses.*

But it wasn't too long after that that I began to notice that the print on the children's prescription bottles was getting smaller. And then I discovered that I couldn't sit down and sew a button while watching the television. I had to remove my lenses or glasses to see the needle and thread, but then I couldn't see the TV. I considered wearing my glasses taped to my forehead so that when I looked up I could see distance and when I looked down I could see the needle and thread.

The road to middle age seems to be paved with compromises. Eventually I had to bite the bullet and admit that I would need reading glasses some of the time, just for really tiny print, only when wearing my contacts. I comforted myself with the knowledge that I could still lull myself into relaxation at night with a good book and no glasses or contacts at all. (Please don't tell me that that, too, will be changing soon.)

The big day arrived. I would be selecting my first pair of reading glasses. But where were my friends to come with me and give me pointers on what to look for and how to use them? I was alone for this traumatic milestone.

I approached the display three times, each time getting a little closer. Finally I said to myself, *Well, come on . . . what am I going to do, stay here all day? Eventually my family will come home, and after a few hours they might start to wonder where I am.* I can see the headline on the cover of a supermarket tabloid now: "Woman Found Paralyzed at Reading Glasses Display."

Another woman arrived to try on reading glasses. I could tell she wasn't a novice. I took courage from her example and approached the display for the coming-of-age ritual. There were demi-glasses and full glasses. I ignored the demi-glasses. To me they screamed "over-the-hill," and they reminded me of something Mrs. Santa Claus might wear.

I picked out a pair of full glasses in a frame similar to the pair I already own (for nearsightedness). I tried them on. They were very strong, even for the mildest correction, but yes, I could see the fine print on the chart and read it too. I looked at my thumbnail and realized that I could see it clearly, even with my contact lenses in! I looked in the mirror to see how they looked. Talk about instant motion sickness! I could not see myself; all I could see were psychedelic shapes and colors in motion. I took the glasses off instantly and was relieved to see everything return to normal. I turned to the woman. "How are you supposed to see what you look like in these?"

She looked liked one who is weary and has given up on certain things in life . . . like knowing what you look like in reading glasses. And she gave me a look that said, "Don't ask. You'll find out."

I took the glasses. At home I tried reading aspirin bottles and ward lists. I set them on my desk next to the magnifying glass. I answered questions all week long on whose glasses those were and why. I allowed family members to see what I looked like in them, knowing I'd never know.

Okay, so now I've passed through that ritual. I just need to find out one more thing. Now that I've got two pairs of contact lenses, several pairs of sunglasses, one pair of glasses for chronic myopia, contact lens solutions and cases stored all over the place, glasses cases, a magnifying glass, *and* reading glasses . . . I'd just like to know, where does it end? Can I stop here? Or will I find myself with all kinds of glasses stored all over the place, including a pair or two on a chain around my neck? Will I be saying, "Wait, I forgot my glasses," to which my children will reply a patronizing pat, "But Mother, you haven't forgotten your glasses; they're right here on your face." And to which I will indignantly respond, "Not *these* glasses . . . my *reading* glasses!"

And does it progress from here to other assorted items which I will need to keep about my person at all times, until I can't go anywhere without looking like I'm in the luggage business?

As a preadolescent I had preteen magazines and all my friends to fill me in on what to expect, in a joyful, giggly sort of way. Now I must be extra observant as I watch whoever is just a step ahead of me as she silently goes through the various milestones of reaching the "golden years."

I wonder who was watching me at that reading glasses display. Whoever it was, I'll bet she won't even try to see how she looks in reading glasses.


I didn't quite know what I was doing when I tried on those reading glasses. I also didn't know what to expect when I first began to teach Relief Society. I learned a few things through trial and error, and I gladly pass them on . . .

## *RS Lessons*

I've been teaching in Relief Society for about eight years, so I feel qualified to offer some pointers on the subject:

• Supposedly there will be thirty-five to forty-five minutes for your lesson. In reality there will be twenty-eight minutes. Prepare for sixty minutes.

• If you are nervous you will talk faster and you'll run out of lesson material after fifteen minutes.

• If no one raises her hand to share related anecdotes, you'll run out of lesson material after fifteen minutes.

• If the lesson material is especially lofty, dry, or difficult to comprehend, prepare double the amount of material.

• If the lesson is on parent-child or spousal relationships, gossip, or aging, you need only prepare four to six topic sentences. The class will take over from there.

• Visual aids are a personal choice. Some teachers seem to choreograph a Broadway extravaganza-worth of visual aids. This may be excessive. But one puny poster on curled butcher paper with a few anemic lines scrawled on it may be better off left at home.

• Keep in mind that one of the purposes of visual aids is to give the teacher a chance to unlock her knees and stretch as she puts the visual aid in place. It's very important to keep the blood circulating back to her brain where she will need it.

• When you call upon sisters to help you present material during your lesson, you might be inclined to call on those sisters who already tend to be the most visibly active participants. And they will say, "Oh, I'd love to, really. But you ought to call some of the sisters who have not been so involved." At which point they will produce for you a list complete with phone numbers. You will find that when you call upon these sisters they will be out of town, not home, or on their way to visit a sick relative, or they will say, "No, *no!*" Then you will call the sisters you originally called, and since it has come to be Saturday, you will *beg*. Some of them will take pity on you and agree to assist you, but you will spend Saturday evening rushing to their homes to give them the material and you will be apologizing for waiting until the last minute.

• When preparing your lesson and materials it will be wise to have a plan A, plan B, plan C, plan D, and so on. You'll need to shift to another plan when:

—The sister who was to sing gets tonsillitis.
—The copy machine breaks down and there will be no handouts.
—Sunday School goes over and you must cut fifteen minutes from your lesson.
—Sunday School gets out early and you must add fifteen minutes to your lesson.
—A visual aid insists on giving in to gravity.
—You get something under your contact lens.

• Sneak into the Relief Society room early and hide all your materials behind the piano. If you don't, you'll be like a fish swimming upstream, struggling with your boxes, posters, and easels as the Sunday School mob makes its agonizingly slow way out the doors, socializing all the way. By the time you make it into the room you'll look like you were playing football and you'll be clutching at crumpled posters just as your lesson is announced.

Those are just a few pointers of the temporal sort. Now for a spiritual pointer. Pray a lot before your lesson—that you will teach by the Spirit in order to deliver exactly what it is that the women will need to hear. There's no way for you to know what that is otherwise, and even if your visual aids are by Rembrandt, it won't help unless you teach by the Spirit, and, oh yeah, don't talk too fast; you'll sound like Minnie Mouse.

# PART FOUR

❖

# You Can Run but You Can't Hide

*(The Self Versus Nature)*

One of the mightiest struggles of life takes place between the self and nature. Just ask the middle-ager who is attempting to zip up a pair of jeans, is reaching for a pencil that has fallen under a chair, or is trying to keep strawberry-colored lipstick from climbing vertically in little streaks. We can run but we can't hide.

The ironies are everywhere, threatening to catch us. For instance, in middle age we discover that it becomes necessary that we read food labels very carefully. It could be that we have accumulated some allergies over the years; it is even more likely to be our cholesterol levels, our sodium intake, our fat intake, or all of the above. Whatever the case, we are told to read those labels religiously. And we discover that just about the same time it becomes required that we read the tiny labels . . . we can't.

Is there no justice? Why is it that our eyes could focus near and far with equal ability in the days when we could eat saturated chemicals all day long and not be affected in the least? Did we care about labels then? If we couldn't laugh, we'd cry, and never get anything else done.

About the only thing that makes sense about middle age is that when we reach this stage of irony, we have usually developed a few traits to enable us to survive the stage.

One of the traits we have gained is an ability to make the most of what we've got, especially time. We don't like to waste it, but we also don't like to cram it tightly with many pieces like a jigsaw puzzle. We learn to savor our moments and go with the flow . . .

## The Darkened Theater of Life

My husband and I went to see a comedy at one of those cheap theaters, the kind that charge $1.50 per seat and you pay for the rest of the ticket by tolerating a sticky floor and having your knees crammed into the seat in front of you.

On this particular night we were enjoying ourselves as Steve Martin was just about to fall into a pool. Suddenly there was an abrupt cut to the next scene. It was obvious to all in attendance that this was not creative editing that we were witnessing, but a damaged print.

The audience was quick to express their reaction to the loss of those few frames that would've shown us the big splash and its aftermath. There was an uproar. The sound was huge and full of groaning, grumbling, and complaining. I could understand the audience's reaction.

It was only natural that the audience would be miffed. But what disturbed me was that they continued with their loud complaining long after the movie continued into the next two scenes. Enough is enough. So we missed the highlight of a scene; shall we also miss the next two scenes as well? That I couldn't understand.

There were the characters continuing with the plot, and we were all missing it due to the choice of the vocal complainers. We couldn't do anything about the missing scene, but after that, it was our choice.

We often do that with life too. Something bad, horrible, or tacky happens and we carry it along with us until even the present becomes contaminated by the past. And then we can't enjoy the present either. Life goes on without us, and we're missing it.

Or we may have something looming on the horizon: a root canal, an appointment with the principal, a medical procedure, April fifteenth, or even vague uncertainties, death, becoming a bag lady, drought, famine, and pestilence. Then our expected future ills contaminate our present.

With this stuff crowding in from both sides, we haven't got much of a present left. And if we have no present, then when shall we live? The time will just tick away without us.

There's enough material out there for us to gather and create and/or prolong negative experiences. Why, one painful surgery could keep us miserable for years after.

And life goes on. If we're too busy grumbling or worrying, we'll miss it. So enough already, quit your bellyaching and watch the movie!


It's not just your imagination. Things *are* speeding up. You *are* on a treadmill. But you can get off. At least occasionally . . .

## *Limits*

It seems that the older I get, the hurrieder I get. It's been challenging balancing the many balls in my juggling act over the years. In years past there were babies and all that goes with them (like carrying them everywhere you go, even into the bathroom) that I had to juggle along with work and school-age kids and church responsibilities.

Now there are no babies, but that is more than made up for with teenagers. I may not have to take them everywhere I go, but I ought to. Some of the balls I am juggling are smaller, but then, some of them are now larger, and there are more of them.

Because I frequently—no, make that always—do more than one thing at a time, I have found that in most cases three things at once is my limit before there is a noticeable falling off of performance quality. For instance, I can be doing my daughter's hair, giving my son a spelling test, and making dinner all at the same time. But if I try to do my daughter's hair, give my son a spelling test, make dinner, and get a zipper unstuck simultaneously, there will be considerable stress to the system.

Because I have learned this about myself, I have from time to time—no, make that extremely often—told my kids when they have come to me with a homework problem or a tangled shoelace that "I am already doing three things at once and that is my limit" so they'll have to take a number and I'll get to them when there is an opening. Apparently at least one of the kids was listening one time when I said this. My daughter Kiera must have given some thought to the concept of simultaneous multiple activity. She was about eight or nine when she called to me, "I'm doing more than three things at once!"

I was passing her room carrying dirty dish towels out to the laundry area and soda cans to the recycling bin on my way to get the sheets out of the dryer while quizzing a son for a social studies test. But I couldn't resist. I stopped to witness her feat. Could she outdo me? It had taken me years to master my juggling style.

I stopped at her door. She looked up at me and recited, "I'm breathing in and out and my heart is beating and working and my mind is working and I'm growing and I'm wiggling my legs like this."

I smiled sweetly and said, "That's nice." Then I went into the garage and put the dirty dish towels in the recycling bin. I had to admit, there was something for me to learn from her "expertise." Why had I never put breathing on my "to-do" list? Perhaps I should pause and see if there is any growing going on while I'm at it. I always wondered if I could find some method for checking off more items on my lists. If I include breathing, or being and growing, that's two or three things I'm already doing. Aren't these things as important as dusting?

I put everything down and went into Kiera's room. I sat next to her and we wiggled our legs together. When my son came into the room and said, "Mom, can you drive me to David's?" I said, "Sorry, I'm already doing more than three things at once. As soon as I finish one of them I'll let you know."

He looked at me like this was the moment he'd seen coming for years. Mom finally went round the bend. If only he knew.


Holding still is a necessity to invite gratitude. I remember a story about some people who were traveling through a jungle with the help of hired natives who carried some of their belongings. The group made haste through the jungle and after a while noticed that their helpers were no longer with them. They went back and found them sitting. When asked for an explanation they said that they had been moving so quickly through the jungle that they had to stop to let their souls catch up with them.

One of the paradoxes of middle age is that we get in a hurry and must stop to catch our souls. And yet at the same time, it is a time when we begin to face our own mortality. For instance, when one turns forty-five it's pretty hard not to notice that if one doubles that number, one comes up with ninety. And that means, for those of you too young to care, that one has reached and passed the midpoint.

Though I have often pondered and written about the concept of living life fully, I never really truly had to face the possibility that I may not be around much longer until a medical crisis forced me to. The experience was both the most terrifying and the most peaceful of my life . . .

## *Time Bomb*

"Well, it looks like you're walking around with a time bomb in your head." This is what my internist told me. This is not the kind of thing you want to hear from a doctor. Let me explain.

It all began with a sensation like a spider crawling across my chin. It was five days before Christmas, so I was pretty busy addressing cards, wrapping things, and trying to get my kids to calm down. For a couple of days I kept feeling the sensation and kept reaching up to brush the phantom insect away.

Soon the left half of my face and then the left side of my head became a circus of strange sensations: stabs, prickly sensations, and a feeling like hot water spilling across my face.

When the sensations spread to the other side of my face and then to all the rest of my body, I became seriously concerned. When I began to have trouble walking, I became terrified.

I was rushed in for an emergency MRI. On the MRI they found an angioma, which is a type of vascular malformation. The neurologist suspected that a previous injury of some kind had caused the malformation.

Thus began many weeks of tests, including an EEG and an MR-angiogram, and many weeks of fluctuating between terror and peace. I had to face the fact that my life was hanging in the balance. I was warned that the threat of a brain hemorrhage was a possibility and that if it were to happen it was likely I wouldn't survive it.

I looked at my life and my family in a different light. I saw everything as fleeting. I experienced tremendous sadness. I wished to have a chance to raise my children. I experienced anger. I said to myself, *What good is it to enjoy the present wonderful moments or to count my blessings if I'm not going to be here much longer?*

After the anger and sadness and turmoil there was a struggle of faith. Did faith mean I should ask to be healed and know that I would? Or did faith mean I should quietly accept the will of the Lord no matter what it might be?

Eventually, through much personal prayer, the prayers of others, and spiritual experiences, I arrived in a place I'd never been before. It was a place of precious peace. I realized that there are many things about earth life that I would like to leave behind. I thought of my dad, who died in the midst of my medical crisis, and wondered if he was preparing to meet me. I decided that my Heavenly Father knew where I was needed the most and that I could trust in His decision. I experienced a delicious kind of homesickness, a longing for home.

Once I entered this new place, all was well. Every second became magnified with meaning. Every sound, every breath, and every single hint about the other beings in my life became precious. I was more truly alive than I had ever been before. I had been divinely kissed. I knew it was a precious blessing. I was not afraid to die. And I was utterly alive.

Six months later, after a medical conference in another state, I was told that the vascular malformation in my brain, though somewhat risky, was not the kind to portend imminent death. There was some other neurological disorder going on which caused the symptoms and led to the MRIs.

I felt both joy and sorrow at this news. The reason for the joy is obvious—I had been given my life back. The sorrow needs explanation. In the weeks that followed I found that my biggest struggle was in holding on to the precious perspective I gained when I was facing death.

It has become valuable to me to recall that I have experienced some physical healing during this course of crisis. I know that I have also experienced spiritual healing. During the darkest moments I was often blessed with divine intervention to guide me back toward hope. And the love of friends and family was like a tangible support upon which I could lean.

But no matter what happens, I have experienced a trial that has taught me. I no longer wish to hurry through my life. I now plan to do those things that are the most meaningful to me. And I see how valuable my family is to me. I am quieter now, and more centered. I watch people getting crazed over trivial matters. So much doesn't matter in the eternal perspective.

Sure there are difficulties. Dealing with a mysterious neurological disorder is but one of them. But hey, this isn't just an existence, this is an adventure!

When I wasn't sure how long I'd have to live, I thought of what messages I wanted to give my children. Primarily it would be that I have a testimony and that I love them. I'd want them to know that I would always love them and that I would eagerly await my reunion with them. I'd want to photograph them more. I began to write in my journal more. I noticed that when someone spoke to me I felt as if I were peering into their soul.

I was more patient with family and strangers. I found the things my husband did were more endearing and less annoying. I found myself, after getting over the sadness and anger, in love with life and everybody in it. I found myself in a better place than I had been in before. Or at least, my view of things had improved.

It's a precious, peaceful perspective that is difficult to

obtain and keep. I am the same person then and now; why should it be so difficult to achieve this kind of peace? It shouldn't matter whether a doctor tells me I have a time bomb in my head or not. Life is fleeting and precious for all of us.

## *Falling Apart*

I was at a baby shower, wearing a wrist brace. Of course, I was asked about fifty times what had happened, and fifty times I replied that I had pulled a ligament while lifting my bike up onto the bicycle carrier.

Thinking about how these kinds of things didn't happen that easily before, and thinking of the many ways I was experiencing the indignities of little injuries, I explored a little further with the next woman who inquired.

"I think I've discovered the age when it all starts to fall apart," I said. I was thinking 44.5, but she responded, "Well, for me it was age twenty-nine."

"Oh," I said, struggling to put some of the delicious brunch on my plate with one arm, and wondering what the fat content was. "What makes you think I'm *not* twenty-nine?" I was just being silly, but several of the women looked at me then, so I felt compelled to continue. "Yeah," I said, "I had my first child when I was six years old. There I was, on the cover of the *National Busybody,* a puzzled look on my face. It was in all the supermarkets."

I went to find a seat; I didn't think I could hold the plate much longer. My elbow was also hurting. My husband said it was tennis elbow. That was an irony that wasn't amusing. I hate tennis.

At home we have a collection of slings, crutches, neck braces, and now wrist braces from the many and varied injuries we've sustained. There's a Snoopy sling from when my daughter broke her wrist. And there's the neck brace that I tolerated for about two hours after being rear-ended four years ago. My daughter's wrist is like new now. My trapezius muscles, however, will never be the same.

I imagine that if I continue to collect these little muscle pulls and tears and sprains I will be able to accurately forecast the weather, but I may not be able to ride my bike, which would make me very crotchety.

When I was a child and saw an elderly person struggling to move his body, I thought it was simply a matter of the aging process. But now I see it is more likely a result of the living process. They say that when we come to the end of our lives we will find ourselves to be the sum total of our experiences. I used to think of that as character formation. Little did I realize how much we will also be shaped by our physical experiences.

If only I could concentrate more on the character forming experiences and eliminate the body deforming ones. These days when I am driving in rush hour traffic (which is difficult to avoid around here) and I see, in my rearview mirror, a vehicle approaching too rapidly as I am stopping for a red light, I go through several stages of coping. First I think, *No, not another whiplash! I'll lose all mobility I have left!* Then I brace my head against the head rest, hoping there is a way to minimize injury. And then I think, *Well, we don't have a video camera yet.*

But I suspect that even if I lived in an area where whiplashes were rare, there would be something else that would nick at my mobility. There's no denying it. As my spirit becomes more and more mobile, as it comes closer and closer to being able to soar, my body will become more and more stiff. It's just one of those paradoxes about life that are so unfair. Just as I am becoming, internally, a Christie Brinkley in a red Ferrari, I am appearing to be, externally, a Mrs. Cubbison in an old Buick.

It would be truly depressing if I couldn't imagine that I might experience eternally a coming together of body and spirit in a limitless, soaring fashion.

When we're seventeen we lack many things because we haven't yet experienced enough to form them—things like maturity, mellowness, peace, perspective, and a seasoned sense of humor. When we're eighty-something we have soaring spirits—unless we've spent our lives pursuing vain things, like youth. In between, those middle years, we make the choices that determine our final product. But inside every wizened lady in sensible shoes is a girl dancing in a flowered dress . . .

## *Eternally Seventeen*

*Originally written as a script for an RS lesson. Elderly woman sits feet up or rocks in a rocking chair; concentrates on reading or crocheting. Looks up and sees Relief Society sisters gathered before her. She is startled.*

Oh, hello, sisters! How nice of you to pay me a visit!

If you'll excuse me, I think I'll just rest here for a moment. My son and daughter-in-law just brought me home from a visit, and I'm a little tired.

You probably think I'm tired from my grandchildren whooping and hollering like the little savages they are. But that's not it at all. No siree. Those savages have fire! And they're honest too!

My four-year-old grandson said, "Grandma! How come your hands look like a lizard's back?"

I said, " 'Cause I'm old! But my hands don't feel like a lizard, do they?"

He crawled into my lap and said, "No, they're soft, like an angel's wings. Are you an angel, Grandma?"

Before I could answer, my daughter-in-law whooshed in and interrupted all the fun. In one breath she said, "Now, don't you go bothering Grandma like that. You kids clean up this mess and get into bed right this instant, you hear?"

Young people are always in such a hurry these days. Off they went and there I sat, empty-lapped and surrounded by bossy adults! Not only do they tend to spoil my fun, they're taking away my independence!

They say I can't drive anymore. So I drove the wrong way down a one-way street! Everybody makes a mistake now and then. They think that proves I'm not fit to drive. But you don't see them taking the keys away from my sixteen-year-old granddaughter . . . the one who ran into a parked car!

If they take away my car, how will I drive to the hairdresser's so Reggie can continue to make me beautiful? How will I get to Evelyn's to play Scrabble?

And I know what will be next. They're going to want me to move out of my home. I know where everything is here. It took me forty-five years to get everything just where I want it, and finally there's no one to move things where I have to search for them!

Maybe I should just throw a temper tantrum and refuse to do what they tell me to do. They treat me like a child; why not act like one?

My daughter-in-law tells me not to go into the den. She's afraid I'll fall down the one step into the room. Okay, so I fell there once. That's because I didn't know there's a step there! I know there's a step there now! I don't fall in the same place twice!

Then they talk really loud to me. And really s-l-o-w-l-y. I know my hearing is not like it used to be, but my hearing doesn't have anything to do with my thinking. I'm not getting dim-witted.

The other day I was shopping for a birthday gift for Evelyn. I forgot all about being old; I was having so much fun looking at the new spring dresses all covered in flowers. Then I accidentally passed a mirror. I wondered who that old lady was. What a surprise! It was me!

I don't know how I got to be so old. It seems like just a few months ago I was seventeen and dancing in a pretty spring dress.

Well, I've been babbling on and on. I understand you've got a Relief Society lesson here tonight. It's about helping the dependent adult, right?

Can you please be sure to mention:

—How important it is to have some kind of autonomy, especially at my age.
—That I have a mind and it's full of all kinds of special things. I've had lots of experiences, you know. My memories make some pretty funny stories.

—That I won't be trying out for the Olympics anytime soon, but there are still things I can do to make a contribution. I want to feel useful.

—And that I want to be acknowledged for all my experiences, and who I've become as a result.

Oh, and don't forget—deep down inside, I'm still a young dancing lady in a flowered spring dress!

*Dances off slowly, humming and smiling.*

I've got a few more decades in which to learn before I reach the lofty octogenarian stage. I'm already getting an inkling of what it will be like due to the many external signs of aging, such as the Halloween I helped my daughter create an authentic costume from a period in history, from memory. She was a hippie. And one of the other parents looked her over and said, "That sure is an authentic costume. Your mom must've saved some things from those good old days."

And recently Erin, the teenage girl next door, came over to interview me about what it was like the day that President Kennedy was assassinated. She told me I was the only person she could find who was old enough to remember it. Her parents were too young.

When I told her I was in a high school English class when I heard the news, her eyes widened with elder respect. How can this be? How can I have so much history to recall? I'm still young. Is it bulging history that pushes our short-term memory out of place? I wish I could remember where the time went. Even more, I wish I could remember where I put the keys . . .

## Absentminded

Some friends of mine were talking about how scary it was that they were getting to be so absentminded. As far as they were concerned, dementia was just around the corner. One friend said she didn't want to be a babbling bag lady on some corner telling passersby that of all the things she'd lost, she missed her mind the most.

I tried to reassure them that they were not losing it. They just had more things on their minds. Potty training, after all, was confined to one dimension. Teenagers with car keys thrust us into a life that more closely resembles a multilevel video game full of thrills and spills and requiring the player to be mega-alert. One might tend to forget where one put the bananas under the circumstances.

Perhaps I felt a little defensive too. I've had a tendency to be a little absentminded myself. But this is not something new that has come with age; I was that way even when my mind was fresh and free, uncluttered by the needs and emergencies of a family who saw me as the all-purpose clearinghouse.

So, to reassure my friends (and myself), I've devised a list of symptoms to let them know that they are well within the range of normal. For instance:

- If you forget where you put your car keys, that's normal. However, if you forget what car keys are for, you might want to pay attention.
- If you find yourself standing in front of the open refrigerator wondering what you opened it for, that's okay. If you see your shoes sitting on the top shelf, it could be a symptom to consider.
- If you can't remember your kids' names, you're okay. If you completely forget that you have kids and get upset when you realize that all those kids coming in the door and grabbing food are yours, you may be headed for trouble.
- If you rush into the living room with a sense of purpose, only to forget what the purpose was, you're normal. But if you rush into the living room with a sense of purpose and realize you're two houses down, you've got a problem.
- If you walk out of the grocery store and can't find your car, it could be because you simply forgot where you parked (or you live in a metropolis and it's stolen). No problem. But if you look for hours and call one of your kids to come get you and you are taken home and there's your car, right in the driveway where you left it, this could be a mild hint at what's to come.

You can forget your wallet, drive four hundred miles without your license, leave your son at the gas station, forget the name of your best friend of thirty-five years, forget to pick up your husband when you promised just five minutes ago . . . but you're still okay as long as you remember this one thing:

Yes, just this one important thing. It will make all the difference in the world. You'll rest assured that you are normal and all is well . . . and you're okay. Give me a minute, it'll come to me; it's right on the tip of my tongue.

And I'd tell you what that is, only I can't seem to remember what it was I was going to say. Hey, who is that kid? Why, he's walking right in the door and walking over to the refrigerator! Who does he think he is? Hey! Kid!


Those of you who know and love a middle-aged person know that they require special care during these difficult and critical years. You need a guide. At last, here it is . . .

## *Care and Handling of a Middle-Aged Person*

Middle age is a difficult time. Middle-agers are not young enough to be foolish, carefree, and smooth of skin and body. And they aren't senior citizens, so they can't be eccentric or wise, and they can't get discounts on anything either.

Middle age is a kind of limbo. It's neither here nor there, and there aren't any obvious advantages. Considering that this is a period of vast waistlands, hormonal nightmares, and identity crises, those who are not in this stage of life ought to consider more effective ways of relating to those who are. Consider the do's and don'ts of the care and handling of the middle-aged person in your life:

**Don't** say to a middle-ager (hereafter referred to as an MA), "But you don't look old enough to have grown children!" Not only is this ploy overused, it will not be believed by the MA. The MA will find herself in the awkward position of having to explain to you why she indeed is old enough to have grown children. Her choices are limited to: (a) "Not only am I old enough to have grown children, I look old enough." (b) "Are you suggesting that I dropped out of tenth grade in order to begin a family?" (c) "They're actually my younger brothers and sisters; don't tell anyone. When our parents died suddenly, I promised that even though I was only twelve I'd never let anyone take them away. I've been secretly raising them all these years." Or (d) "You're right, I'm not old enough to have grown children."

**Do** accept that the MA doesn't feel compelled to hide her age or accomplishments and doesn't feel it's the eighth wonder of the world that she has grown children. She does feel it is a stage she has achieved after much hard work, late nights, and countless tears and prayers.

**Don't** say to the MA, "You look pretty good for someone your age." Statements like this cause the MA to imagine that you think she ought to look like "The Mummy"!

**Do** find something to compliment the MA about. Even though no MAs look like Jane Fonda except Jane, they all have qualities worth mentioning. They could have nice eyes, nice hair, or a nice backhand, or they may be exceptionally good cooks or silversmiths.

**Don't** shy away from subjects like, "What was it like in the fifties?" MAs and senior citizens alike would never want to erase their life experiences in order to seem younger. What would be the point of that?

**Do** check your history, however, before you blurt out your ignorance. You will want to avoid asking an MA what it was like, for instance, before there were schools or cars.

If you are young, **don't** assume that the MA won't be able to do something that is physical. Today's MAs are baby boomers ("We are boomers, hear us roar, in numbers too big to ignore. . . ."). They originated the school of fitness. Be careful; you might not be able to keep up with the MA.

If you are older, **do** allow for the fact that the MAs are now middle-aged, and although they may have been painting daisies on their foreheads and singing "Where Have All the Flowers Gone?" that was a lo-o-o-ng time ago, and the flower children have been through car insurance and parent-teacher conferences since then. But **don't** expect them to be exactly like everyone else. They never did get a taste for polyester.

**Don't** stereotype today's MAs. Growing up in a generation this huge, they have had to value individuality just to survive. The middle-aged lady coming out of the supermarket with a bag of cat litter probably has a black belt in karate. The balding man at the library probably writes incredibly intricate, poetic mysteries that have won literary prizes.

**Do** ask the MA in your life what she thinks about world affairs, current events, current movies and books, and the latest fad among the junior high set. She will be much more comfortable discussing the news or a book than defending that she is old enough to have grown children.

And whether you are younger or older, consider that the MAs of today have been through quite a bit in their lives, including an assassination of a president, a war that took many of their too-young loved ones throughout all their coming-of-age years, and the Beatles. Consider that they may have some wisdom. But also consider that they are still struggling to grow up and understand it all.

When you reach middle age you learn to truly appreciate the fine art of taking a break. And so here comes one . . .

## *Quake Surfing*

In the wake of the Northridge quake of January 17, 1994, we Southern Californians, trendsetters that we are, have invented a new sport called "quake surfing."

If your home is on or near the epicenter (the center of all the rocking and rolling, where the quake is the strongest, for those of you who haven't experienced a quake . . . yet) you cannot even attempt this sport, nor should you even try. All your energy will be focused on survival, as well it should be. But not to worry. The next one could be somewhere else.

For optimum quake surfing conditions, one must have an epicenter either near a television or radio station, or a television or radio station must be between you and an epicenter.

For example, the Northridge quake was centered in the San Fernando Valley, which is northeast of us. We are here along the Orange County coast. Hollywood is between us and the San Fernando Valley, making for perfect quake-surfing conditions.

At the first big shaker, none of us could quake surf, however. We were all tossed from our beds at 4:31 A.M.—not a favorite time to be awakened. In fact, we began to refer to this one as an "earthwake," and when we watched the news later and saw that many politicians were coming from Washington for photo ops, my son, Michael, said, "Someone should warn them that every single person in Southern California was awakened pretty early today and we're all going to be grumpy."

We were fortunate that, after checking our gas line and water line, we were able to settle down in front of a television and wait for the Richter scale reading and epicenter results to come in. Our house shook considerably, but the only thing that happened (besides a sudden impromptu meeting in the center hallway well before dawn) was that some books and things keeled over. I kept waiting for someone to ask how we did in the quake so I could say, "Well, as you can see, the house is really a mess!" But I'd eventually have to admit that most of the mess was made by my children the night before.

Others were not quite as fortunate, of course. There were many tragedies and lost lives. Most of us were somewhere in between. We called my mom, who lives much closer, too close, to the epicenter, at 4:40 A.M., and we made contact several other times in the days that followed. Each time we spoke she was busy cleaning up bits of glass and china.

After speaking to her the first time, we continued to wait to hear the facts, several of us making our predictions as to the magnitude and location of the quake. I thought of the list of phone calls I was planning to return that day and thought I could maybe make good use of the time and start to return those calls; after all, I was guaranteed that they'd all be awake already. But I didn't (don't worry!), because we're not supposed to tie up the telephone lines after an earthquake.

So we sat and waited. Some of us climbed back into bed, and some of us sat in rocker-type chairs, which we noticed tended to turn aftershocks into amusement-park-like rides. And that's when we began to learn to quake surf.

As we watched the news the newscasters would stop mid-sentence each time an aftershock was felt, and suddenly on the screen there would appear a seismograph with a little jerking needle describing the size of the aftershock. We discovered that since the newscasters in Hollywood were feeling the aftershocks before we did, we had our own little built-in earthquake warning system. We could get up and go about our business and wait for them to announce an aftershock. When they said, "Uh-oh . . . here comes another . . . yes, it's another aftershock; ohhhh, it's a good one," we'd get into whatever place we wanted to be to ride it out. It would take several seconds for us to feel a toned-down version of what they were feeling northeast of us.

It wasn't long before it became a sport. We'd try aftershocks in rocking chairs, outside, horizontal on linoleum, leaning against the kitchen counter, standing in the middle of the room with our eyes closed, and in many other positions and locations—never by a window, however. (Do not try this in your state; we are experienced quake surfers.)

Of course, our neighbors in the San Fernando Valley had no such warning system. And in any case, they felt most of the aftershocks while waiting in line for water or forms for disaster relief. They couldn't get any enjoyment out of it at all. But as I said earlier, next time the quake may be centered in Orange County, and by then the valley inhabitants will have their electricity restored and they will be able to watch as the Hollywood newscasters say, "Whoa . . . here come's another one," and we'll be standing in lines because our water supply is buried in a pile of rubble. At least now that they have read this they'll know all about quake surfing and will be able to get something out of the experience while they put their books back on the shelves and express gratitude that that's the worse that happened to them.

As fellow residents of the south of California, it's the least we can do to share each other's trends as well as miseries.

Oh, and just one more thing: We keep hearing from people who are presently living in the tundra (the Rockies and eastward). They are asking, as if we must be particularly dense out here, "Why do you Californians insist on living out there where there are earthquakes all the time?" They are shivering while they ask this, as it is 10° below, without taking into account the windchill factor. I guess all this sunshine has just fried our brains or something.

There. Now that we've had some recreation, time to move on to more serious matters, like how to determine when one has reached middle age . . .

## *Stages*

There is debate over just exactly when it is that one reaches middle age. There's a theory that says that middle age is always ten years older than you are, which one can use for many years, up to a point.

One can continue to push the envelope, but unless one comes to accept (after doubling one's age, perhaps, and facing some realities) that one is, indeed, middle-aged, there could be some problems with semantics and ages and stages. It might look a little suspicious, for instance, if one were to spend only a year or two in middle age and claim to be a young adult up until that moment. Suddenly getting discounts on haircuts shortly thereafter might also add to the suspicion.

One must learn to go through these various stages with full awareness and some kind of elegance and style, if not wholehearted acceptance. And in order to fully realize one's stage, one must realize that one is in a particular stage.

Fortunately (and I use that word advisedly) there are some telltale signs to indicate that one has, indeed, reached the dubious stage known as middle age. For instance:

- One might discover that the concept of a night with nowhere to go and an early bedtime is irresistibly alluring.
- Upon visiting a college campus, one might wonder why there are no college students present, only what appears to be a bunch of junior-high-age kids.

- Rising early one morning, one might discover a rather prominent pillow crease across one's cheek—not a new experience, of course. But when it is still there, just as prominent, after lunch . . . now, that's another story, and middle age can no longer be ignored.
- When going out for the evening and expecting the hubby to say, as he has in previous years, "You look nice," one may notice that instead he is saying, "You have lipstick on your teeth."
- As ironic as it may seem, one of the most significant signs is the tendency to forget one's age and to find oneself in the doctor's office being asked just that by a nurse, and then finding oneself asking the (young) nurse a stupid question like, "What year is it?" so one can make a quick calculation.
- One might find oneself requesting that one's kids pick up something off the floor because one would like to avoid bending over, and then one will wait for an undeterminable amount of time, silently thinking that if one had not asked, one could've picked up the item and been done with it already.
- It might be wise for one to be prepared when looking in the current textbooks at the next back-to-school night. One might discover that the history textbooks are covering a period of time in which one was a college student.
- If one is too curious, one might discover that some of the parents of the classmates of one's youngest child are about the age one's eldest child would be if one had had him when one was twenty-two. One might wish to distract oneself at this moment before one considers the implications of that—that one is old enough to be a grandmother to one's youngest child's classmates (and one's youngest child!?).
- When one goes out in a tunic top, one is no longer taken aside and asked if one is expecting.

There are, of course, many other symptoms to watch out for. For instance, one may not be able to eat as much as one used to without consequence, the wedding clothes no longer fit, and one wouldn't recognize one's high school classmates if they all marched together down the street wearing uniforms in the school colors with the name of the school and the date of graduation embroidered in gold.

But even with many obvious symptoms, middle age can sneak up on one who is either unobservant or wishing, however subconsciously, to deny its approach. If one is not observant, the arrival of middle age may come as a shock.

Pay attention to those little signs of middle age. Note them and learn to accept them, one by one, line upon line. One must begin with milk before one can eat meat. It's easier to digest that way. And besides, at your age, you really can't take such a shock.

Shock and stress can take their toll when one gets to be of "uncertain age." To combat such things one might consider controlling one's thoughts, which is easier said than done . . .

## *Looks*

I saw a promo for a talk show that promised to feature a bevy of "over-forty beauties" giving away their secrets. It got my interest. Especially when the camera panned along the row of them, all looking like they'd just turned fifteen or seventeen. If for no other reason, I was curious to find out how they managed to look so healthy and glowing. I taped the show and it only took me two weeks to find a moment to watch (while I was getting some exercise indoors on a stormy day).

They were generous with their secrets. They talked about drinking lots of water (I took a long swig from my water bottle). They talked about getting enough sleep (I made a mental note to find my seventeen-year-old a ride to seminary). They said that rest is very important (I considered who to put in charge of grocery shopping). Next they talked about exercise and how important that was to their well-being (I huffed and puffed).

Then they discussed stress. They said that stress must be

minimized. I knew they were right. But I wondered how that was done. Perhaps if one is a former supermodel one can preserve one's already exceptional looks with lots of rest and little stress because one has hired an entire team to interface with reality, and to take care of groceries, too, while they're at it. But, emerging feelings of skepticism aside, I still was willing to listen, because they made some sense.

And then they talked about such things as attitude and how the way one feels on the inside shows on the outside. *So true,* I thought, and I tried beautifying my insides with my thoughts. The last commercial break came. When they came back, a member of the audience asked them a question about plastic surgery. With only three minutes of the program left, every single one of the "over-forty-beauties" not only admitted to but listed all of their cosmetic surgeries. All of them.

So, I learned the secret of their forever young looks. And I'm trying really hard to do something about the way I am feeling on the inside right about now.

I usually try to look at the silver lining in every cloud. Try as I might, I can't think of what the silver lining might be in seeing those ladies talking about all their plastic surgeries, except maybe we ought to be grateful that we don't feel compelled to pay the costs of that kind of maintenance, even if we could afford it. There are other things that are much more valuable, are there not?

## Firestorm '93

When I heard the weather reports predicting several days of Santa Ana winds, I groaned. We Southern Californians know these winds well. They come at us, hot and dry, from across the desert. Our skin and sinuses turn into parched riverbeds. Everyone complains of allergies, contact lens wearers are in agony, our plants look like they've been hit with a blowtorch, and our kids get crazy. Okay, crazier. We all get tense and shriveled.

Someone once named the Santa Anas "devil winds." It doesn't surprise me. When the humidity drops and the winds come, it is officially fire season. I have grown up with fires because my hometown is in the foothills of the Angeles National Forest. If you have ever experienced, as I have, walking home from school along Foothill Boulevard with a canyon fire to your left and a hillside brush fire to your right, you would understand why someone would call the Santa Anas "devil winds."

However, all my experience with fire seasons didn't prepare me for the firestorm of 1993. Living these days in Huntington Beach, our natural disaster concerns are earthquakes (frequent), hurricanes (occasional), tsunamis (rare), and tourists (always). We are not in a brush fire area here, so when the fires started in the foothills on October 26, our concerns were for those relatives still living in those areas.

But fires kept breaking out all over. Soon there were nearly twenty major fires burning out of control in five counties. How could we be of any help to relatives in the foothills if we were surrounded by fires ourselves? We watched the news, mesmerized. Soon Laguna Beach was engulfed and we saw entire neighborhoods burning to the ground. A canopy of smoke hung over us, darkening the sky. It snowed ashes, and soon the car was covered in them. We watched a large propane tank explode on TV. It made a loud pop, and a mushroom cloud formed. About three seconds later we heard the actual explosion. We ran into the backyard to see the mushroom cloud on the horizon.

The fires raged on, and there was nothing we could do but watch helplessly as house after house was reduced to ashes. Sometimes we saw flames form into tornado-like forms and rush across the hills. Never in my life have I ever seen such intensely violent flames. It was not only helplessness we were feeling but some underlying fear. When would it stop?

Although we were apprehensive for many reasons, we kept talking and found ways to relieve some of the stress with humor. When we talked about what causes Santa Ana winds (a high pressure system over Utah), one of us said it was Utah's fault that we were on fire. My seventeen-year-old, Michael, quickly added, "Yeah, the Utah Saints are trying to hurry the Second Coming!"

Our television sat in its alcove, showing nothing but fire twenty-four hours a day for days. There weren't even any commercials. Usually the TV is on only for limited hours on the weekends, but in this case we kept it on to keep us informed about where the fires were and where they were headed. After a while we began to refer to it as our fireplace. We've never actually had a fireplace, so we were struck by how much our television had begun to resemble one. There were fluctuating flames and crackling sounds; we could even smell the fire. Of course, the smells and the ashes came in through our windows, and from time to time we saw lots of little firefighters running around in our fireplace, not to mention the helicopters making water drops.

We'd go about our business, stopping from time to time to see what was happening. And most evenings we'd gather together around our "fireplace," watching as if hypnotized by the flames. But we had to go to bed eventually, uncertainty intact.

By the time we'd concluded that life would have to go on, including some sleep, there was a fire advancing closer to our neighborhood. The community of Turtle Rock, near the University of California, Irvine, was being evacuated. Turtle Rock is about twenty minutes from us, and there are several large communities between, so it was highly likely that we would not be evacuated. But the theme of the day had been "unpredictability." The firestorm that rapidly raged through Altadena had not been fully anticipated. The fire in Laguna Beach had begun as a small brush fire and was expected to be put out immediately. Most of the fires had changed course suddenly, one overtaking a fire truck and sending experienced firefighters to the hospital with critical burns. The "devil winds" were whipping the fires about, making their progress unpredictable. Stopping them was nearly impossible.

While we could tell our children that we probably wouldn't need to evacuate during the night, we couldn't make any promises. I debated about what I should tell them. They were already worried. I decided to be truthful and tell them to pack an overnight bag, a "flee bag," just in case. Into it they put a change of clothes, comfortable shoes, toothbrush, and any memento that would be irreplaceable. At bedtime my daughter told me she felt better after packing a bag. *There,* I thought, *doing something can take away some of that helpless, fearful feeling.* Then she told me that she was looking forward to feeling stupid for packing it as she unpacked it the next morning.

After the kids went to bed I packed my backpack. After putting in my shoes, change of clothes, toothbrush, and prescription sunglasses I added my Walkman, driver's license, water bottle, and several bandannas (in case we needed to wet them and wrap them around our mouths and noses). As I collected these essentials into the one backpack I saw the other things I'd want to take if I had the time: the photo albums, the computer disks, my camera, a favorite pair of shoes. I began to see all the things I had that enriched my life, instead of the things I wished I had (like a video camera and a decent pair of boots). Then I saw all the things that make our lives comfortable that would be lost if our home burnt down: telephones, computers, refrigerators, blankets, towels, and garbage disposals.

But even as I was seeing how much we have that we'd hate to lose, I was also aware that we could just walk out with only ourselves, empty-handed, and we'd still be richly blessed. It was an empowering feeling to realize that if we were notified in the night to leave immediately, I could walk out with just one backpack, if that much. It was possible to leave so much behind and walk out. Our lives are the only true essentials. We could travel much lighter than we do. We could give it all up. The backpack packing exercise calmed me. I felt that no matter what happened, we would be okay.

The next morning we were glad that the fires hadn't reached our community, though we felt sorrow for those who'd awakened to find their neighborhoods nothing but blackened stubble. The entire experience was horrifying, even from our relatively safe distance. The sky was orange, ashes covered everything, and we had headaches and stiff necks from the tension of a restless night.

My thirteen-year-old son, his face contorted by a migraine, said it all. "Mom," he said, "I woke up this morning and looked around and I felt rich. I don't know why, but I just felt rich."

Yes, we're rich. Our lives are incredibly rich with blessings and choices and things to do. But around middle age we begin to catch on that we really can't do it all . . .

## *Time*

Is it just me, or am I hurrying faster and only getting more and more behind? With so many obligations and so many children, my days feel like an overpacked can of sardines. I feel like I'd need some kind of giant shoehorn to squeeze in one more thing.

I can't wait for another time to have some time. I've got to find a way to have some time now, when I don't have any time.

Through trial and error, I've learned a few things. I've learned:

• If you wish to eat a semi-peaceful dinner—as peaceful as it can be considering the table is full of kids and their friends, Dad is at work, and several of the kids need to be at a youth activity in fifteen minutes or they'll be left behind, and several of the friends need to be taken home—let the answering machine answer the telephone. That's why you bought it. And deny dessert to any kid who picks it up while you're eating.

• It does help to schedule in blank spaces on your calendar. These are supposedly so you can have some breathing space, but even when you do this your schedule will end up being tight (which makes you wonder what it would be like if you didn't schedule in some blank spaces).

• Allow for emergencies. You never know when the school will call to let you know that one of your children seems to have broken something, like a bone (their own or another's).

Allow about three hours per week of flexible time per child. That doesn't mean you'll be sitting by the phone, keys in hand, for that time period. (It won't happen then anyway; these calls only come when you're in the shower, or in the middle of something especially messy, requiring that you wear old, grubby clothes.) Just be sure to be involved in more flexible kinds of things every so often so you can shove everything aside if you find yourself in an emergency room for about sixteen hours some days.

• Learn to say no. Begin with just a simple "n." Take a deep breath and try another "n." If you can't do that, learn some other tactics, like truthful excuses. For instance, say: "I've got a family member here who is sick; I have to take care of him." (You just saw the dog vomit in a corner of the yard.) "I was just on my way out the door." (The kitchen door.) "I have an important meeting that night." (With myself; I think I've forgotten who I am. If I don't attend this meeting, who knows who I'll be?) "I'll be out of town that weekend." (I'll be out of my mind; isn't that far enough?)

• Learn what's important to you and let the rest of it decay in heaps all around you. So the oven never gets cleaned. Eventually you'll need a new one. It'll be clean. In the meantime, in the time you could save by not cleaning the oven, you could learn to play a musical instrument, make a quilt, read lots of good books—all memorable things. The only person who would ever notice the inside of your oven, or remember it, is a person you don't care to know anyway.

• Imagine that you will die in six months (I hate to tell you this, but do you have any guarantees you won't?). What do you want to be doing? How do you want to be remembered? Do you want to go down as a spotless housekeeper? Or would you like to get in a little skydiving (okay, then, a cruise might be nice) and write a funny poem that your grandchildren will quote?

The other day I was driving in traffic, taking a son to school. All about me were drivers who desperately wanted to be the first ones to arrive at their jobs and would cut off their mothers to do it.

When I am in traffic like that, I've learned that the best

thing to do is to take a deep, cleansing breath and to allow just a little more space between me and the traffic in front of me. On this particular day as I did this and saw the frantic drivers pulling into my sanity-saving space, I turned to my son and said, "Time is like driving in traffic. If you allow enough space, someone will come along and fill it."

"That's profound," he said, a bit sarcastically (he's a teenager). "Are you going to put that in one of your books?"

"Yes," I said, "I think I will." And so you see, Michael, I have. But what it is that I'm trying to say is that time management may not be the answer. It seems that the answer is, to ask ourselves what is the best use of our time and our talents and what are our dreams and then to just *do it* before someone else comes along to fill in the blanks for us.

In middle age it is time to weed our gardens and determine what is significant and what isn't.

Perhaps middle age could be considered to be the great equalizer, a time to become humble. It's certainly a time when our experience and struggles teach us perspective.

Perhaps the purposes of middle age are all that we have explored thus far, and perhaps this time is a transition from temporal existence to eternal existence . . .

## *A Temporal Versus Eternal Comparison of Aging on Planet Earth*

Middle age is a time to face reality. The fact that we will not be immortal youths for the rest of our lives is faced every morning when we look in our bathroom mirrors. Ask any woman who goes to put on her makeup and drops her mascara when she sees her mother looking back in the mirror. Ask any man who discovers he has more chins to shave.

Middle age is also a time to get things in perspective either as a symptom of maturity or as a tool for survival. If we see our lives primarily from a temporal perspective, we will increase in discouragement as our waistlines increase in love handles. However, an eternal perspective will give us an entirely different point of view:

|  | TEMPORAL | ETERNAL |
|---|---|---|
| The newborn | beautiful | a fresh spirit but wrinkly, helpless, dependent, selfish |
| The child | shiny-haired, soft and smooth, lots of energy | learning, making mistakes, self-centered |
| The teen | metabolism that won't quit, unbounded energy and passion | making many mistakes, self-involved, moody, emerging |
| The young adult | prime of life, beautiful, strong | under pressure to decide, much to learn, mistakes to correct |
| The adult | beginning to fade | learning humility |
| The middle-ager | first realization that one will physically fall apart | humble, learning to serve, emerging gratitude, free from previous limitations |
| The senior adult | definitely falling apart | actively serving, loving, with an attitude of gratitude |
| The elderly | wrinkly, frail, helpless | beautiful |

If we can see life as an ongoing process in which one doesn't merely get older, but better—much better—perhaps we will better tolerate the creaks and groans, the sags and bags, the forgetfulness, the teenagers and young adults and our tempestuous days. Perhaps we should see our gray hairs and wrinkles as badges of courage, ribbons of honor, purple hearts.

In middle age one of the things we learn is that we often view life with the grass-is-greener filter, which blinds us to the present. When we are young parents, groggily changing a cheerful infant at 3:00 A.M., we look wistfully upon our young adult years and wonder if we took full advantage of those years. When we are teens we see adulthood as the ultimate in carefree freedom.

Keeping that in mind, it might be good for us to look for the advantages of middle age and to magnify them. I will do that the moment I remember what they are.

And when we get to our senior, sunset, golden years, we might be able to find joy then as well. Maybe we should proudly flaunt our white hair as much as we flaunt our grandchildren. We should consider our worn and wrinkled skin like a well-used, well-worn leather that has served us well and grown more beautiful with use. We should have our hands photographed. When we are reunited with perfected bodies, we might miss the accurate story our worn bodies could tell! We might hope that we made the most of those last years and endured, fully and joyfully, to the end.